LEARNING
TO LOVE

FINDHORN CLASSICS

LEARNING TO LOVE

EILEEN CADDY, MBE, AND DAVID EARL PLATTS, PHD

FINDHORN PRESS

Findhorn Press
One Park Street
Rochester, Vermont 05767
www.findhornpress.com

Text stock is SFI certified

Findhorn Press is a division of Inner Traditions International

Disclaimer

The information in this book is given in good faith and is neither intended to diagnose any physical or mental condition nor to serve as a substitute for informed medical advice or care. Please contact your health professional for medical advice and treatment. Neither author nor publisher can be held liable by any person for any loss or damage whatsoever which may arise from the use of this book or any of the information therein.

Cataloging-in-Publication Data for this title is available from the Library of Congress

ISBN 978-1-62055-835-5 (print)
ISBN 978-1-62055-836-2 (ebook)

Printed and bound in the United States by Lake Book Manufacturing Inc.
The text stock is SFI certified. The Sustainable Forestry Initiative® program promotes sustainable forest management.

10 9 8 7 6 5 4 3 2 1

Edited by Michael Hawkins
Text design and layout by Damian Keenan
This book was typeset in Adobe Garamond Pro and Calluna Sans with Bernhard Modern Std used as a display typeface.

To send correspondence to the authors of this book, mail a first-class letter to David Earl Platts c/o Inner Traditions • Bear & Company, One Park Street, Rochester, VT 05767, USA and we will forward the communication.

Contents

Preface

First things first. "The garden came second, Findhorn began with the inner voice." Eileen Caddy was clearer than the purest crystal you may find that it was this way round. All that has grown from sandy windswept soil – the thousands of visitors, the growth of a community of 500 souls, an Eco-Village, workshops, conferences, came from a longing to connect with and follow the beloved voice within.

On first reading this updated manuscript of *Learning to Love,* myriad images, sounds, sensations and smells washed through me: candle smoke in the yellow-seated sanctuary, the coconut-infused aroma of the Gorse bushes that flower in April/May and garland The Park, and a host of different languages that fill The Park and Cluny Hill College.

How much has changed since this book was first published in 1993. And how much hasn't. All that has grown from the day Peter, Eileen and Dorothy Maclean arrived at The Park – effectively the town's rubbish dump – has followed from their dedication to finding and following the still small voice of divinity within themselves.

Let's not be coy about this. The Findhorn Foundation Community, in all its sparkling multi-faceted aspects, has grown through a remarkable dedication to love. It may be a word that is difficult to shout from the geodesic roof of the Universal Hall, since it can be freighted with flakiness, yet love has been the guiding star. In 2012, the year the Findhorn Foundation and community celebrated its 50th Birthday, a special conference was held: Love, Magic, Miracles.

As co-focaliser, I remember writing, in my proposal 'that for millennia spiritual teachers, including Findhorn founders Eileen Caddy and Dorothy Maclean, have proclaimed this truth. And now, at a time in our planet's evolution when all of humanity is facing extraordinary challenges and opportunities, more than ever before, love is what we truly need.' We quoted co-founder Dorothy Maclean, "In my life I have learned one great truth; that love is the greatest power on earth. This statement has been tested time and time again."

Fast forward to 2018 and it is generally accepted that the world is in a perilous state; recently the doomsday clock was even moved a few moments closer to midnight.

I would suggest learning to be more loving is a positive step any of us can take at this time, or any time or place. And despite external appearances in the world to the contrary, I can hear Eileen Caddy with her faith and trust firmly in the Divinity Within herself, saying, "All is in God's Hands, and all is very, very well."

Over many years Eileen and David Earl Platts ran workshops centred on learning to love, and the exercises, rooted in the principles of psychosynthesis, and Findhorn's founding three graces – love, magic, miracles – explored the blocks to love and how to overcome them, starting with ourselves.

I am delighted this wonderful 'roadmap' with its exercises, meditations, guided by Eileen and David has been updated and revised. The book was distilled from their workshops. Thousands came to them and it is an abiding regret that I didn't attend one.

⌒

During my two-decade-plus stay in the Community I did meet Eileen, of course. I was at the MBE (Member of the British Empire) investiture ceremony, in 2004, representing the Communications Department where I worked at the time, editing the Foundation's Newsletter, *Network News* and often holding the PR fort.

My job was to be with the Press and photographers and ensure they didn't overtax Eileen. In the foyer of the Universal Hall, the Lord Lieutenant of Morayshire pinned the award on Eileen while flashbulbs popped. At one point a feisty local reporter was getting too close and sharp with Eileen. Unfortunately for me he had sharp elbows too, so I couldn't restrain him. Eileen stopped, raised her head and said, "I'd like a cup of tea, please." A cup of tea duly appeared, the journalist drew back, and harmony was restored. Phew.

Another time I interviewed her for the Foundation's internal magazine, *Rainbow Bridge*, and she told me how in the early days she enjoyed opening and closing the sanctuary curtains at beginning and end of day. Nothing was too mundane for her. There have been many stories of people asking Eileen questions and receiving helpful, sometimes profound, if not life changing, answers. I too, hesitantly, asked her something and…

she didn't answer. She gazed at me silently. I will never forget her gaze. (And the answer came.)

I met David Platts in the early 1990s when he and others were guiding new Foundation members through the basic principles and techniques of Psychosynthesis. Cultured, mannered and deeply grounded in spirituality and psychotherapy, David was held in very high regard by people in the Community. I watched him guide us through a 'practice session' and I was struck by his deep humanity, intellect and grounded spirituality. And not least for me, his old-fashioned courtesy and respectful approach.

In the intervening years we have all gone through changes and the FF Community is almost unrecognizable. It is, rather grandly, an NGO associated with the United Nations Department of Public Information, holder of UN Habitat Best Practice designation and is co-founder of the Global Ecovillage Network and Holistic Centres Network. It is a thriving community and eco-village and has a retreat centre on the sacred Isle of Iona. And it continues to be a mystery school.

True to its sandy roots and continuing the journey started by its founders, the Findhorn Foundation hosted, in 2014, the New Story Summit: Inspiring Pathways for our Planetary Future. This was a multicultural enquiry into a new story for humanity, attracting activists from over 50 countries. The New Story summit aimed to contribute to the next phase of humanity's conscious evolution.

Most importantly, we end as we began. The Foundation's website states, unequivocally… 'where everyday life is guided by the inner voice of spirit'. No change here. First things first; learn to love.

Michael Hawkins
Forres, 2018

Accredited Counsellor (MBACP), facilitator of therapeutic/personal transformation groups and member of the Findhorn Foundation community for more than 25 years.

What Is the
Findhorn Foundation?

The Findhorn Foundation Community is a dynamic experiment where everyday life is guided by the inner voice of spirit, where we work in co-creation with the intelligence of nature and take inspired action towards our vision of a better world. We share our learning and way of life in experiential workshops, conferences and events that take place within a thriving community and ecovillage.

The Foundation has two main sites. The Park, nestled amidst dunes and forest, bay and beach, is an ecovillage that is home to many of our staff and a larger community of people living with shared values. Cluny Hill is a stately Victorian former hotel, five miles away from The Park, which houses staff and welcomes participants in our workshops and events. Our retreat house on the island of Iona, and the satellite community on the neighbouring island of Erraid, also welcome participants for life-changing experiences on the wild, wind-swept west coast of Scotland.

The Findhorn Foundation is an NGO associated with the United Nations Department of Public Information, holder of UN Habitat Best Practice designation and is co-founder of the Global Ecovillage Network and Holistic Centres Network. The Foundation is at the heart of a community of more than 500 people who every day support and live the vision of creating a better world by starting with themselves.

For more information visit www.findhorn.org or email bookings@ findhorn.org

What Is Psychosynthesis?

Many of the principles and techniques in this book derive from Psychosynthesis, a holistic educational and psychospiritual approach to human growth and development. It was created by the Italian psychiatrist Roberto

Assagioli, MD (1888-1974) who formulated steps to achieve harmonious inner integration, true self-realization and right relationships.

Unusual contributions of Psychosynthesis are:

- Recognition of the essential transpersonal or spiritual nature of human beings.

- The high value it places on intuition, creative insight and inspiration.

- Development of the Will as a psychological function resulting in personal empowerment and greater capacity to make and implement life-enhancing choices.

Psychosynthesis creates a positive atmosphere for self-exploration: a guiding principle is to accept and redeem patterns of behaviour, rather than to judge and negate them.

It helps people to understand and master their problems, improve their relationships, realize their creative potential, contribute within a wider social and planetary context and explore life's meaning and purpose.

Psychosynthesis holds that to love well calls for all that is demanded by the practice of any human activity, namely an adequate measure of discipline, patience and persistence. It suggests that self-mastery begins with self-knowledge and self-understanding.

Refer to the *Recommended Reading* list on page 123 for further information.

Introduction

The authors have developed a step-by-step strategy based on the following principles to help people learn to love themselves and others.

- While love takes many different forms, a useful working definition of *love is compassionate acceptance of and respect for ourself and others.*

- As *human* beings, we are born with the full capacity to love. It is our God-given heritage, a divine spark existing within everyone, a spark which can be found and fanned into a brightly burning flame.

- As *spiritual* beings, we are pure love, with a need to express our basic nature: to love, to serve, to feel wholeness and oneness with all life.

- As a self-defence in response to painful experiences we have had, we have erected protective barriers within ourself which also prevent love from flowing freely in and out. We have developed fears, resistances, beliefs and patterns of behaviour which keep these barriers firmly in place.

- The primary lesson in life is to learn to love. It is why we are here on Earth, and thus it holds the highest priority on our time and attention. No other lesson is as important or as necessary for us to learn.

- We cannot love others until we first love ourself, and many of us do not love ourself or others very freely, fully and fearlessly.

- A basic reason many of us do not love ourself is because of doubts we have about our own sense of worth, having formed very early in life a negative belief about ourself such as, 'I am not good enough', 'I can't do anything right', 'I am a failure', 'I am inadequate' or 'I don't deserve love'.

- We can *choose* to accept and respect ourself and others. We can *choose* to change our beliefs and behaviour. We can *choose* to take down our barriers, and experience love's natural flow within us.

- Learning to love is learning how to make these choices and how to put them into effective action. Choosing requires an intention to change and a willingness to take action. Personal empowerment and a greater sense of freedom come from making choices.

- Helping us to make and implement these choices is a loving, pure, permanent centre of Self-awareness, love and will deep within ourself which animates and directs our life.

- We always stand at a crossroads where we have the choice to bring more love into our life. It is a choice which often has to be made over and over again, day by day, moment by moment.

- Our choice to be more loving may be facilitated by learning and applying relevant personal awareness principles and techniques, many having their origin in Psychosynthesis, a holistic, person-centred approach to human growth and development introduced by the Italian psychiatrist Roberto Assagioli, MD (1888–1974).

This book invites you to make free and informed choices—ones which will nourish and nurture you—and then helps you put them into action clearly and confidently each step of the way.

We suggest you take your time with each chapter, doing the exercises and suggestions before proceeding to the next chapter. Pace yourself. Resist the temptation to read this book from cover to cover as fast as you can. Learning to love is a process to unfold, not a race to be won.

1

Choosing to Allow

In this first chapter we explore the meaning of love and present a few simple ways for you to begin to bring more love into your life.

What Is Love?

The word love means different things to different people. It is sacred to some and meaningless to others. Yet everyone has an inner response to love in one way or another.

Some of us use love to refer to sexual desire. Others use it to describe feelings of affection and romance. Some people use it to reflect appreciation and caring. Still others say it is the universal principle of attraction and union.

How do you feel about love? What is the meaning of love to you? Consider for a moment how you usually use the word.

One way of defining love is to describe what it is and what it is not. Perhaps you have just now used this method yourself. Such a description of love appears in the Apostle Paul's First Letter to the Corinthians, 13:4–8:

> "Love is patient and kind; it is not jealous or conceited or proud; love is not ill mannered or selfish or irritable; love does not keep a record of wrongs; love is not happy with evil but is happy with the truth. Love never gives up; and its faith, hope and patience never fail. Love is eternal."

For many of us love is an elusive and emotionally charged word having a variety of meanings. As you proceed through this book, you may find that your definition of love changes.

Reality of Love

The following statements suggest a range of beliefs people hold about the reality of love.

- 'Love does not exist on this planet. It is like "security", a word used to describe an ideal state which I find conspicuously absent in life.'

- 'Love has been expressed in the world by a few special teachers, such as Buddha, Jesus, Krishna, Mohammed and Moses, but it is quite out of reach to us mere mortals.'

- 'I notice other people expressing love, but I am not sure I have ever felt it within myself, and so I have some personal difficulty in relating to it.'

- 'I know I am capable of giving and receiving love, and I can feel it within myself and many others.'

- 'I try to love freely, fully and fearlessly to the best of my ability.'

- 'I am pure love. All else is only fear, illusion and talk.'

How about you? What is your belief about love? Is it one of these statements? A combination of them? Or something entirely different?

Defining Love

We, the authors, have each had a lifetime of lessons about love, some of which we are still learning. Do understand that we are not putting ourselves forward as experts and saying we have all the answers. Far from it. An adage says people teach what they most need to learn. We were sure it was not by accident that we have had our own learning about love to do for many years at the Findhorn Foundation and elsewhere.

What is love? We hear about it. We speak about it. But what does it mean? Love is one of the most misunderstood words in the dictionary. Love is not just a word. It is an essence. It is a vibration. It is a power. It is life itself.

Love is the most priceless energy in all the universe. Why? It is because love overcomes all fear. Love is the balm which contains the power to heal and renew. It is the key to every door.

As we open our heart, we begin to understand the true meaning of love. A closed heart knows nothing of love. We can know love, we can feel it, and yet we cannot hold on to it, for the more we try to possess it, the more it eludes us. Love is as free as the wind and knows no limitations or barriers. True love is never possessive; it never holds another person in bondage, but longs to see every soul free and unfettered, finding its rightful place in the perfect scheme of things. With love comes freedom. It is fear that binds and limits; it is love that cuts away all bonds and frees.

Love is not something which can be bought, sold, or measured. We can only give love. Love is in everyone and everything in varying degrees and is waiting to be drawn forth. Love is not something apart from us; love is who we are. We are born with the capacity to love and be loved. Each of us is here on Earth to express love to ourself and to one another.

Answering the call of love demands much courage and determination because vulnerability always includes a risk of being rejected. But without vulnerability love is impossible, and without love, life is incomplete.

Love is the indescribable, powerful energy flowing through our whole being out to all our fellow men and women, enabling us to see beyond their outer form to the Divinity Within each one, creating within us a feeling of oneness, wholeness and the *peace of God which passes all understanding*.

While love takes many forms, we have learned the most important form of love is self-love—not egotism, but rather self-acceptance, self-appreciation, self-esteem. Without it, we cannot genuinely and fully love another person. We only remain needy and look outside ourself for confirmation, validation and love.

Acceptance and Respect

We use this working definition: "Love is compassionate acceptance of and respect for ourself and others."

Thus, choosing to love means learning to take ourself as we are and others as they are. It means learning to respect ourself and others. It means acting with compassion, caring, warmth and understanding.

What about emotions, romance, feelings—where do they fit into a definition of love? Philosopher Martin Buber says love "is not an emotion or a feeling. Feelings accompany love, but they do not constitute it." Theologian Millar Burrows also suggests love "is not an emotion but an attitude of the will ... To love one's neighbour is not to feel affection for him but to wish and seek his good." Clearly, love is more than just a feeling.

As a personal yardstick for ourselves, we define love even more simply by saying to love is to allow. The extent to which we are able to allow ourself to be as we are—that is, to accept ourself and others without judgement or criticism—is the extent to which we truly love.

We can choose to accept and respect ourself and others. We can choose to allow ourself and others to be as we are. Therefore, we can choose to love, and we can choose to bring more love into our life.

Pure Forms and Distortions

The quality of love can be experienced and expressed in many ways. Some ways can be considered pure, while others are distorted through our needs, desires and experience. The following list gives examples of both forms. To get a sense of love and how you relate to it, consider for a moment how often you experience or express each of these qualities.

Love

Pure Forms	Distortions
• Acceptance	• Attachment
• Compassion	• Conformity
• Cooperation	• Dependence
• Inclusiveness	• Exclusiveness
• Openness	• Fear of rejection
• Receptivity	• Jealousy
• Respect	• Neediness
• Sensitivity to others	• Possessiveness
• Trust	• Self-centredness
• Union/Unity	• Sentimentality

Ladder of Life

The humorist Mark Twain says, "Principles don't mean much on an empty stomach." His statement, later to be echoed in the writings of psychologist Abraham Maslow, suggests we have different kinds of needs, and a priority exists whereby some needs have to be satisfied before others can be met.

Thus, the principle of love (and the attendant need for acceptance and inclusion) will not mean much to us until we have taken care of more basic needs. Food in our stomach. Clothes on our back. Roof over our head. We have devised the following simple ladder of qualities which puts love into context with other personal needs.

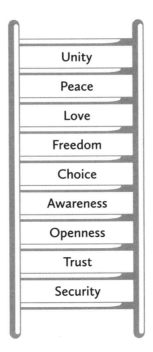

Unity

Peace

Love

Freedom

Choice

Awareness

Openness

Trust

Security

We devote separate chapters in this book to each of the first seven qualities. The issue of Chapter Two, *security,* comes first on our ladder. We usually have to feel safe and secure before we are ready to venture out, to dare, to risk. Once we do feel safe, however, then the quality of *trust* becomes more available to us. It is difficult (but not impossible) for us to trust when we do not feel secure, and easier to trust when we do. Our ladder also suggests we have to trust *before* we can love.

Trust then leads us to the third rung, *openness,* that is, being frank, unguarded and vulnerable. It is difficult for us to be open if we cannot trust—ourself, others, life, God. Having trust frees us to be honest and open.

The more open we are, the more aware we can be. The opposite is also true: the more closed we are, the more unaware we are of what is happening in our life. Therefore, the next rung of our ladder is *awareness.*

With awareness comes the power of *choice.* As we become aware of our behaviour patterns and blind spots, we have the choice to continue them if we feel they serve us, or to change them if they are too limiting. Our choices can then become more deliberate and life enhancing rather than unconscious and limiting.

Choice leads to greater *freedom.* How do we know? When do we not feel empowered and free? It is when we feel we have no choice. Thus, making and implementing a choice in any matter liberates, empowers and strengthens us and keeps us from feeling stuck, victimized or helpless.

Freedom opens the way to *love,* the seventh rung of our ladder. We can love only when we feel free, that is, when we are not limited by anxieties, fears and the behaviour patterns they create.

Love fosters *peace.* It is difficult for us to feel peaceful in the absence of love. Feeling love for ourself and others creates the peace.

Peace brings us a sense of *unity,* an interconnectedness with humanity, with all life, with the God Within at the very centre of our being.

NOTE. This sequence of qualities is not altogether a linear, step-by-step process. For example, openness may lead directly to freedom: the more open we are the freer we usually are. Note also we can be on one rung of the ladder in one part of our life, such as in our work, and on a completely different one in another part, such as in our personal relationships.

EXERCISE: *Learning from Experience*

Short exercises are included in each chapter to help you experience for yourself relevant aspects of each topic. This exercise shows how to use past experience to gain new awareness. If you pre-record it, it will help you when you play it back to experience it more freely and fully without interruption. When you record, read the text quite slowly and include ample pauses in which to take the action suggested. Pause 10–30 seconds, or whatever length of time seems comfortable and appropriate, at every set of dots (...) to allow you to experience each step fully. Avoid rushing through the exercise. Take your time.

> *Close your eyes... Sit up straight... Take a few deep breaths... Relax....*
> *Allow your body, emotions and thoughts to become still... Become like a calm, quiet lake...*
>
> *When you are ready, allow to come to you a memory of a time when you felt very loving... Your love may have been directed towards yourself, another person, an animal, an object, a cause, or something entirely different...*
>
> *It may be a recent experience, or one from long ago, perhaps even from your childhood...*

*Take your time... Wait patiently in the silence, knowing something
will soon come to you... Be willing to accept whatever comes without
judging, censoring or rejecting it ... Simply be ready to observe and
examine it, with the purpose of learning more about it ...*

*When a memory comes to you, allow specific details to come with it...
Observe and explore the original experience with as many of your senses
as you can... Re-live it ... Let it be very real to you again, but avoid
becoming lost in it ... Then when you are ready, consider the following
questions...*

- How do you experience love?...
- What does loving feel like to you?...
- How does loving register in your body—what physical sensations
  accompany the experience of love for you?...
- How does loving register emotionally—what feelings accompany
  the experience of love for you?...
- How does loving register intellectually—what thoughts, ideas or
  beliefs accompany the experience of love for you?...

Now create a new definition of love, only this time *base it entirely upon
your personal experience of love...* Review your responses to the questions
we have just asked and use them as your own yardstick of whatever love
is to you...

How is it for you to use your experience in this way, that is, as a frame
of reference and as a source of wisdom?...

Make whatever notes or drawings you wish of your experience with
this exercise. Has it given you any new insights or awareness?

Applying It

This final part of each chapter encourages you to use your learning, to lift
it from the pages of this book and bring it into your everyday life. Here are
a few simple ways you can begin now.

1. Models of Behaviour

One way to bring more love into your life is to observe people you admire
who have been successful in their expression of love and note who they
are and how they have done it. The idea is not to imitate them, but
rather to identify the worthy qualities (such as acceptance, compassion,

openness, respect or trust) within them and their behaviour which seem to contribute to their success as loving individuals, and then to find ways to express these desirable qualities in your life more often until they become a natural part of you.

2. Evocative Word Cards

One method of manifesting a desirable quality in your life is to write the name of the quality on cards and put them up in prominent locations in your home where you will see them several times a day: near your bed, on your desk, a door, a wall, the bathroom mirror, the refrigerator. Doing so develops the quality within yourself through subtle programming. With sufficient repetition, the quality begins to be enhanced, evoked and expressed in your life.

3. Brainstorming

Take some time to brainstorm ways you could bring more love into your everyday life. In brainstorming, the point is to allow many ideas to come to you as quickly as possible. Avoid evaluating, judging or rejecting any idea.

Simply write down everything as it occurs spontaneously to you. Then examine your responses. Choose one of them you are willing to act upon and identify a first step you can take to help bring it about. Be specific about when, where and how you plan to do it. Carry on step by step. You may be surprised how easy (or how difficult) it can be.

4. Inspirational Reading

A completely different approach is to read materials about love (both fiction and non-fiction, prose and poetry) which inspire you and evoke loving feelings within you—anything which keeps love an active presence in your life, for then it becomes more real and available to you to draw upon and express.

In each chapter we recommend relevant publications you may wish to read. Here are the first of our favourites.

- *Daily Word,* the monthly Unity magazine (available in British and American editions) offers daily inspirational messages. It is available online.

- *Opening Doors Within,* our own book, presents a short piece of inspirational guidance for each day of the year.

Refer to the section *Recommended Reading* for bibliographic information about these publications.

5. Personal Goal

Select a personal goal for yourself, one relevant action to be taken within the next seven days. Effective personal goals have these characteristics:

- They are simple. Most complex tasks can be divided into smaller, more manageable parts, where successful outcomes are more likely. For example, the goal 'I will learn to love my parents' could begin with the first step of a simpler goal, 'I will write a letter to my parents'.

- They are specific. A goal needs to be precise enough for us to know definitely when we have achieved it. The general goal, 'I will be more loving' would be difficult to assess. The more concrete goal 'I will invite friends into my home at least twice a month' is one which we can verify more easily.

- They describe an action which can be observed. Thus, they require us to do something. 'I will be more considerate of my children' describes an attitude which may not be directly observable, while 'I will read to my children every day' is a demonstrable act.

- They reflect our values, priorities and desires, and therefore, as statements of intention, they have our full, unqualified support.

- They are stated positively and emphatically, beginning with, 'I will ...'

Considering the possibilities, then making a choice, acting upon it and achieving it gives you positive reinforcement, and empowers and strengthens you in the process of bringing more love into your life.

Next in Chapter Two we explore whatever prevents you from loving more freely and fully.

2
—

Choosing to Feel Safe

In this chapter we examine blocks and barriers to love.

We Are Pure Love

This book holds the view that we are fashioned from pure love. Love is who and what we are essentially. Choosing to love, therefore, is choosing to be more of our whole self. It is choosing to accept and respect ourself and others. It is choosing to allow ourself and others to be who we are, without making any judgements or demands.

Therefore, it is not a question of waiting for external conditions— for the right moment, person or combination of events to come along—before we are able to love more fully. We do not have to wait for Cinderella or Prince Charming to sweep us off our feet. We do not have to wait for love to come to us. Expressing love is a matter of choice, a choice which is always ours to make.

If we say we want more love in our life, what stops us from making this choice? The book *A Course in Miracles* states:

> "Your task is not to seek for Love, but merely to seek and find all the barriers within yourself that you have built against it. It is not necessary to seek for what is true, but it is necessary to seek for what is false."

We agree with this observation and base the general design of this book upon it. Therefore, we begin to explore more closely whatever blocks us from making the choice to give and receive love more fully.

Reasons for Not Being More Open to Love

People give different reasons for not being more open to love. The following list offers some typical ones. Have you ever said any of them at one time or another?

- I am very open to love, but the right person has not come along yet.
- I am happy the way I am. My life is very full and satisfying as it is.
- I am very busy now and have no extra time or energy for such things.
- I do not know what love is, so how can I give it?
- I am not lovable.
- I am not good enough. I do not deserve love.
- There is something wrong with me.
- No one could love me if they knew what I am really like.
- I do not know how to love.
- I am incapable of loving.
- I do not want all the bother, aggravation and trouble.
- Men/women only want one thing.
- I am afraid I might be manipulated, used or abused.
- I tried it, and I am never going to let anyone get that close to me again.
- Love hurts.
- I might have to give up my freedom.
- I do not like making commitments. I am not ready for the responsibility.
- I am afraid I might be overwhelmed and lose my sense of self.
- I am afraid I might be trapped for the rest of my life.
- I would rather be miserable by myself than miserable with someone else.
- I cannot trust others.
- I need to be in control to feel safe.
- I am afraid of people.
- My love is too precious to be given away to just anyone and everyone.
- It is not my destiny or karma in this lifetime.

All these statements, as honest and valid as they may appear, actually help us to avoid making the choice to bring more love into our life. They are excuses we give ourself and others, and as such, they become self-imposed limitations.

Childhood Conditioning

As children we usually model ourselves after our parents. We imitate the way they sit, stand, walk and speak. We adopt their habits, likes, dislikes, attitudes and beliefs. Therefore, clues to the way we function as adults can often be found in our early home life and the people who served as models of behaviour.

We find that blocks and barriers to love often come in the form of self-doubts, beliefs and fears which can be traced back to childhood conditioning. We absorbed messages, both directly in so many words (for example a parent who may have said, 'You can't trust people!'), and indirectly through observation of their behaviour (a parent's beliefs or actions which may have conveyed, for example, 'Life is a struggle.').

Often these messages have an accompanying warning, either expressed or implied, which we call 'shoulds' because of the language these warnings usually use: 'You *should* always do this, or you *should* never do that.'

Unless we re-evaluate them later in life as mature, discerning adults, we take these messages and 'shoulds' for granted, and they form our attitudes, beliefs and behaviour which simply continue automatically through habit without ever having been a deliberate choice upon our part.

Consequently, it is valuable to bring to mind an image of the various people and organizations who had a strong influence upon our childhood, such as our mother, father, siblings and other close relatives, teachers, religious leaders, and even people and situations from the mass media, such as radio, television, cinema, video, books and magazines. We can ask ourself, 'What message and "should" about love did I learn *as a child* from this source?' How does that message and 'should' make me feel now *as an adult?*

We can decide which of these messages and 'shoulds' we agree with now as an adult and *choose deliberately and freely to follow,* and which ones we disagree with now and *choose deliberately and freely to discard.*

It is empowering and liberating to distinguish which of our beliefs and behaviours are a result of childhood conditioning, and which are a result of a free and deliberate choice on our part as an adult.

Blocks, Shadows and Fears

The first step in removing blocks is to find out exactly what they are so that we can begin to recognize them in operation. If we remain blind to our blocks, we can do nothing about them, and they continue to have their limiting, sometimes even crippling, effects upon us.

The second step is to accept them as a part of us, and not to judge either them or ourself for having them. (Otherwise we feel guilty on top of everything else.) We need to honour our blocks, our defence mechanisms. They have helped us to cope, to survive. Then when we are ready, we can choose to let them go, one by one.

Some people refer to their inner blocks and barriers as their 'shadow', or the 'dark' side of themselves, making it appear mysterious, even ominous, and difficult if not impossible to master.

We take a more positive approach, guided by Italian psychiatrist Roberto Assagioli, MD, the founder of Psychosynthesis, who says in *The Act of Will:*

> "Many people fear love, fear opening themselves to another human being, a group or an ideal. Sincere and honest self-examination and self-analysis, or an analysis conducted with the help of others, are the means of discovering and unmasking, and then getting rid of, these resistances and fears."

He suggests the way to deal with the 'shadow' is simply to walk side-by-side with it out into the light, that is, into the light of awareness, for therein lies the power of choice. Only as we become aware of our blocks, recognizing and accepting them as a part of ourself, can we then choose to do something about them if we wish.

One purpose of this book therefore, is to show that it is both desirable and possible for you to conduct this 'sincere and honest self-examination and self-analysis'.

We entitle this chapter *Choosing To Feel Safe* because we have found the primary reason most of us do not make the choice to love more freely and fully is that we feel unsafe and insecure in some way about people, relationships, love or even life itself. We fear whatever might happen if we open ourself to giving and receiving love more readily.

What Is Fear?

Fear begins as a thought, anticipating the possibility of an unwanted happening of some kind. The thought is quickly followed by one or more emotional reactions—anxiety, dread, panic, terror—accompanied by feelings of uneasiness, vulnerability and worry.

The following list reflects common fears many of us have. Which ones do you imagine could be blocking you from choosing to love?

- Fear of being abused
- Fear of being hurt
- Fear of being used
- Fear of commitment
- Fear of entrapment
- Fear of failure
- Fear of intimacy
- Fear of losing control
- Fear of losing a sense of self
- Fear of manipulation
- Fear of powerlessness
- Fear of rejection
- Fear of responsibility
- Fear of the unknown

Most of us have such fears. Few of us are totally fearless. Therefore, the task is to recognize our fears and their effect upon us, then to accept them as a part of us and finally to diminish or eliminate their limiting influence upon us. Consider for a moment your response to these questions about fear.

- How fearful are you?
- How much do your fears influence you? How strong are they? How limiting are they?
- When and how do your fears make your relationship decisions for you? When and how do you allow them to stop you from being or doing something?
- What is the worst part of having your fears? What is the best part?
- How do you usually cope with uncomfortable feelings such as fear? What methods do you use to deal with them? What do you actually *do?*

EXERCISE: *Finding a Symbol for Your Fear*

Now we seek the *specific* fear which stops you from bringing more love into your life, for, as we have said, identifying your fear is the first step towards resolving it.

In this exercise you are asked to relax and allow an image or other symbol which represents your fear to come to mind, and then to explore it for the meaning it has for you. Some people feel they simply make these images up in their imagination, and therefore tend not to take them seriously. We believe such images can be valid and have valuable information to give you when you are ready to examine them. For this same reason, we advise giving close attention to your dreams as they may contain useful clues to your growth and development.

You may wish to pre-record this exercise to enable you to experience it freely and fully without interruption. Avoid rushing through the exercise. Take your time.

Close your eyes... Sit up straight... Take a few deep breaths ... Relax...
Allow your body, emotions and thoughts to become still... Become like a calm, quiet lake...

When you are ready, ask yourself the question, 'What is the specific fear stopping me from choosing to love?,... Then allow an image or other symbol to come to you which represents an answer to this question... Take your time...

Wait patiently in the silence, knowing something will soon come to you... Be willing to accept whatever comes without judging, censoring or rejecting it ... Simply be ready to observe and examine it, with the purpose of learning more about it ...

As you begin to sense something, allow it to become more vivid...
Note its size and shape... Its density and design... Its colour and texture...
Explore it with as many of your senses as you can...
Find the overall quality it suggests to you...

Then open your eyes, and express in words or a drawing either the image itself or its quality... If nothing has come to you, hold the question in mind and begin to write or draw freely and spontaneously, letting something come to you in that way... What is the specific fear which stops you from choosing to love?

Reflect upon the overall quality of the symbol and any other words, feelings or thoughts which came to you during the exercise, or you are aware of now.

Make whatever notes or drawings you wish of your experience with this exercise. Has it given you any new insights or awareness?

Functions of Fears

All our behaviour patterns—both the so-called 'positive' and the 'negative' ones—have two primary functions. First, they *limit* us in some way. They hold us back, curtail our freedom, prevent us from changing and growing.

In what specific ways does the fear you identified above limit you?

Second our patterns *serve* us in some way. They help us to achieve whatever we want (such as a sense of security, freedom or empowerment) and to avoid whatever we do not want (such as anxiety, pain or responsibility). One method to find out how a behaviour pattern serves us is to ask ourself what (1) we might lose or miss, and (2) we might have to *do* or *be,* if the pattern were *not* there as a part of us.

In what specific ways does the fear above serve you?

Fear involves a loss of control—part of the fear is that we are either not in control or afraid we will lose control. Fear usually involves another loss of some kind as well. For example, fear of entrapment concerns the loss of freedom. Fear of rejection concerns the loss of self-esteem. Fear of being overwhelmed concerns the loss of a sense of self.

With the fear you identified above, what are you at risk of losing?

Your response reflects the underlying issue which needs to be addressed and resolved before you can feel safe and secure enough to choose to love.

Fear and Taking Risks

Choosing to love means facing our fears and taking risks. A risk refers to taking a chance or gamble on something with an uncertain and even potentially unsafe outcome.

Here is a poem about risks by an unknown author:

To laugh is to risk appearing the fool.
To weep is to risk appearing sentimental.
To reach out for another is to risk involvement.
To expose feelings is to risk exposing your true self.
To place your true ideas, your dreams before a crowd
is to risk their loss.
To love is to risk not being loved in return.
To live is to risk dying.

To hope is to risk despair.
To try is to risk failure.
But risk must be taken because the greatest hazard in life is to
risk nothing.
People who risk nothing, do nothing, are nothing.
They may avoid suffering and sorrow,
But they cannot learn, feel, grow, change, love, live.
Chained by their attitudes, they are slaves.
They have forfeited their freedom.
Only the person who risks is free.

Philosopher Soren Kierkegaard says clearly and simply,

To risk is to lose your footing for a while.
Not to risk is to lose your life.

What do you imagine is the biggest risk you could take concerning love? What makes it a risk for you? What is the underlying issue or concern you have—what could you lose? What could you gain? What would it be like to have more love in your life?

Applying It

Many of us might have the goal always to feel completely safe and secure. But such a goal is an illusion, as life just is not this way—even the most secure and well-balanced people often confront life in unsafe moments.

Therefore, our basic tasks are rather to (1) be true to ourself; (2) create as much security and safety in our life as possible; and (3) accept we can be who we are even if we do not feel safe. It is ultimately a question of priorities and how we focus our attention and energy.

As *A Course in Miracles* suggests, we have blocks and barriers of one kind or another within us. Often it is easier to observe them in others than in ourself. However, as we become aware of our own blocks, we can take charge and begin to diminish their limiting effects upon us. We can begin to take more risks.

Here are a few suggestions for developing your risk-taking capacities.

1. Autogenic Training

By reducing the physical and psychological stress of daily life, we have more attention, readiness and energy to take the risks necessary to bring more love into our life. We have adapted this exercise from *90 Days to Self-Health* by C. Norman Shealy, MD, who credits the original 1930s' autogenic research of J. H. Schultz and Wolfgang Luthe.

> *Close your eyes... Sit up straight... Take a few deep breaths... Relax... Allow your body, emotions and thoughts to become still... Become like a calm, quiet lake...*
>
> *When you are ready, on each in-breath say to yourself (feel the feeling, think the thought), 'My arms and legs are...' and on each out-breath, 'heavy and warm.' Feel the truth of the statement... Know it is so... For two minutes say this statement to yourself over and over again, taking long, slow, deep breaths...*
>
> *Then on each in-breath say to yourself, 'My heartbeat is...' and on each out-breath, '...calm and regular.' Feel the truth of the statement... Know it is so... For two minutes repeat this statement, taking long, slow, deep breaths...*
>
> *Then on each in-breath say to yourself, 'My breathing is...' and on each out-breath, '...free and easy.' Feel the truth of the statement... Know it is so... For two minutes repeat this statement, taking long, slow, deep breaths...*
>
> *Then on each in-breath say to yourself, 'My abdomen...' and on each out-breath, '...is warm.' Feel the truth of the statement... Know it is so... For two minutes repeat this statement, taking long, slow, deep breaths...*
>
> *Then on each in-breath say to yourself, 'My forehead...' and on each out-breath, '...is cool.' Feel the truth of the statement... Know it is so ... For two minutes repeat this statement, taking long, slow, deep breaths...*
>
> *Then on each in-breath say to yourself, 'My mind is...' and on each out-breath, '... quiet and still.' Feel the truth of the statement... Know it is so... For two minutes repeat this statement, taking long, slow, deep breaths...*

Now put all six statements together and repeat ther. five minutes. In subsequent periods, simply repeat turn for a total of twenty minutes. Do this exercise tw seven days, and then notice the difference it begins to t level, sleep pattern, general health and sense of well-beii

2. Verbal Affirmations

Affirmations are positive, seed-planting statements, images and actions which present clearly and precisely a desired outcome as if it were already so.

They are effective techniques used to overcome childhood conditioning. Affirm several times each day (set a timer), *'I always feel safe to choose to love, 'I am bringing more and more love into my life day by day, and 'I am ready and willing to take risks with love now'*. Refer to Chapter Five.

3. Taking Risks

One method of dealing with fears is to confront them directly by taking manageable risks. This exercise helps identify and begin to transform fears associated with taking risks in relationships.

> *Close your eyes... Sit up straight... Take a few deep breaths... Relax... Allow your body, emotions and thoughts to become still... Become like a calm, quiet lake...*
>
> *When you are ready say aloud, 'If I had the courage I would...' and complete the sentence with a word or short phrase—whatever comes spontaneously to you. Do not think about it. Write down the first response which comes. Then do it again, this time allowing a new word or phrase to emerge. Write down the new response. If you blank out momentarily, simply begin again, knowing something will soon come to you. Repeat it again and again for at least five to ten minutes.*

Examine your responses. Note the ideas you feel are worth considering for implementation.

> *Now choose one of them you are willing to put into action within the next seven days. Write it down, beginning with, 'I will...'*
>
> *What makes it a risk for you? What is the fear? What could you lose?*
>
> *What would be the best possible outcome of taking this risk?*
>
> *What would be the worst possible outcome of taking this risk?*
>
> *How willing are you to accept such an outcome?*
>
> *...is important for you to give your full, one hundred per cent support to*

any risk you choose to take. Affirm to yourself, 'I am completely willing to take this risk and to accept its outcome'. Note any feelings and thoughts your affirmation may prompt.

Next find a first step you can take to help bring it about. Be specific about when, where and how you plan to carry it out.

Then take the risk. Put your plan into action within the next seven days.

4. Daily Risks

Ask yourself spontaneously several times a day, *'What risk do I need to be taking right now?'* Whether or not you decide to take a risk is always your choice, but asking the question regularly helps you to become aware of creative alternatives in your life, and keeps you from feeling stuck, disempowered or helpless.

Suggested Reading

- *Feel the Fear and Do It Anyway,* by Susan Jeffers, says taking action is the key to your success in handling fear. Knowing you can handle anything which comes your way allows you to take risks. This book provides many helpful ideas for increasing your sense of personal empowerment and fulfilment.

- *Love is Letting Go of Fear,* by Gerald Jampolsky, MD holds that "although Love is always what we really want, we are often afraid of Love without consciously knowing it, and so we may act both blind and deaf to Love's presence. Yet as we help ourselves and each other let go of fear, we begin to experience a personal transformation."

- *Risking,* by David Viscott, MD, states "If your life is ever going to get better, you'll have to take risks. There is simply no way you can grow without taking chances. When you have an objective worth risking for, your actions become purposeful, and your life begins to make sense, and then no risk can hold you back."

Next in Chapter Three we explore the qualities of faith and trust and how they relate to choosing to love.

3

Choosing to Trust

In this chapter we examine the nature of personal trust and present methods to increase trust in ourself and others.

Spiritual Development

This book places learning to love within a transpersonal context, that is, one in which our continuing spiritual development is an essential part of the process. Psychosynthesis uses the word *spiritual* to refer not to religious matters or to spiritualism but rather to *'all activity which drives the human being forward towards some form of development'*.

Our basic task is to develop a stable, integrated personality by discovering, accepting and transforming behaviour patterns which block us from expressing our full potential. Giving such attention to ourself may be likened to a gardener preparing the ground, digging around and enriching it before the planting takes place.

Then when we plant the seeds of Spirit, they have a more fertile, conducive environment in which to take root, grow and flourish. This transpersonal task, the subject of this chapter, may be likened to the dove of Spirit descending into matter or physical form. It is meant to nurture and support us by providing direction and by expressing a host of pure, universal qualities such as courage, inspiration, joy, love and trust.

What Is Trust?

Trust is a certainty, confidence or conviction in someone or something. Trust believes in, has faith in and depends upon someone or something. Trust develops more easily after our basic safety and security needs are met.

Sooner or later addressing the topic of trust usually brings up underlying questions such as the nature of faith, the meaning and purpose of life and who or what is God. They are big questions and are not easy to answer. However, asking ourself such questions is more important than getting the 'right' answer. Why? It is because our beliefs affect us and how we relate to others, and so it is important to be aware of what we believe. *One principle this book is based upon is that we cannot love others until we love ourself.* In a similar way, we may have difficulty in trusting others, trusting life, trusting God, etc., because we have difficulty trusting ourself.

Personal trust often relates to the beliefs we have about the nature of life. For example, some people believe that everyone and everything in life are part of an organized, trustworthy divine plan which has order, meaning and purpose.

Others hold the opposite view, that is, everything in life happens completely by chance in a totally random fashion, without any such order, meaning or purpose, and therefore without any basis for trust. What do you believe?

Personal trust also relates to faith and the beliefs we have about God. The following statements represent a range of beliefs people hold about the reality of God.

- 'I am an atheist. I know there is no God.'
- 'I am an agnostic. I do not know whether or not there is a God.'
- 'I am a believer. I have faith and trust there is a God.'
- 'I am a human personality, and I have the spirit of God within me.'
- 'I am a pure, divine being, God-like, and I have a human personality through which I express and function.'

How about you? What is your belief about God? Is it any of these statements? A combination of them? Or something entirely different?

Sources of Security, Faith and Trust

Some of us rely on elements in our *external* environment to give us a sense of security: money in the bank, a house, a job, investments or another person such as a parent or partner.

Some of us create life patterns to help us to feel secure and trusting, such as loading ourself down with responsibility and staying busy compulsively from morning to night; or being relentlessly manipulative and needing to stay in complete control of every aspect of our life; or distracting ourself regularly with food, alcohol, drugs, sex and other counter-productive activities to avoid feeling how insecure and unhappy we are.

Even if these externally-oriented manoeuvres succeeded over a long period of time (and they do not), these behaviour patterns cannot provide a very fulfilling life for us. In the end they are only empty cover-ups and compensations, and they do nothing about our underlying feelings of insecurity, fear and anxiety which not only remain untouched, but often continue to grow.

Therefore, in this chapter we explore our *internal* environment and what it offers to provide a sense of security—specifically trust, faith, prayer and the Divinity Within, and how they relate to choosing to love.

Who or What Is God?

One common image of God many people encounter in childhood is that of a Caucasian man with a long white beard in the clouds. Some people think of God as being a benevolent father, always warm and loving, while to others God has human emotions and can be fearsome, angry and vengeful. In either case, God is very human with very human qualities and imperfections.

Other people think of God not as a person but as an abstraction, a concept, a symbol or a quality, such as love, truth or wisdom. Some regard God as an organizing principle, a creator, a source. Still others consider God as simply a body of natural laws in perpetual and impartial operation.

Others say the notion of God is only a convenient fairy tale, conceived to explain the unexplainable, and to make life seem less pointless and more purposeful and worth living. To them God is not a living reality and therefore does not affect their feelings, thoughts or actions.

We find that some people have great resistance to both the word and the reality of God. Like the word *love*, even the word *God* is a very emotionally-charged term for many people. It is also a relatively meaningless word for many others because they have no personal awareness or experience of its reality in their life.

The Divinity Within

We say God refers to who we actually are, our basic essence, our innermost being, our true spiritual self. It is our sacred, unchanging aspect which some people call the Indwelling God, the God Immanent or the Higher Self. Psychosynthesis calls it the Transpersonal Self.

In our books we use either *God* or *the Divinity Within*. It is the loving, pure, permanent centre of self-awareness which is unaffected by our mind's chatter, fluctuating emotions or bodily conditions. It is the vital source within each of us which animates and directs our life.

Our book of spiritual guidance *Opening Doors Within* contains this description of the relationship between the Divinity Within and ourselves:

You are the point of light within My Mind.
You are the point of love within My Heart.
When you can accept it, when you can see yourself
As the microcosm of the macrocosm,
You will never again belittle yourself
Or think ill of yourself.
You will realize that you are indeed
Made in My image and likeness,
That we are one,
And that nothing and no one can separate us.
If you feel any separation from Me,
It is of your own making,
For I never separate Myself from you.
You are individually
What I am universally.
Is it any wonder you have to be born again
To accept the wonder of this truth?
So many souls have strayed so far from Me
And have separated themselves to such an extent
That they have placed Me in the heavens
At such great heights
That I am unapproachable.
I am within you
Hidden in the very depths
Waiting to be recognized and drawn forth.

God Is Love

Some people spend a lifetime in search of God. Searching for the Divinity Within is like searching for the air when all the time we are breathing it. It is like searching for the sun when all the time we are seeing, walking and living in its light.

God is the love in our heart, whatever love we may be capable of expressing presently. To find our Divinity Within, we need go no further than our own kind act or loving thought. As we share our love, we share God with all we meet.

One aspect of bringing more love into our life, therefore, is learning how better to contact, experience and express our Divinity Within.

Faith

Some people use the word faith to signify the religious doctrine they follow, or the church to which they belong. Others use the word to mean belief or trust. Some people use it to refer to the convictions they hold which have no evidence or proof to support them.

We find four principal stages in the development of faith:

- When *we know about God* as an intellectual concept.
- When *we believe in God* as an absolute conviction.
- When *we know God* as an experiential reality.
- When we experience that "the Kingdom of God is within you" *(Luke 17:21),* and not "out there" somewhere, and that we are inseparably one with the divine and, therefore, that *we are God.*

We say faith is intuitive by nature, that is, it perceives the reality of something which is not evident, and then accepts it. *Faith, if nurtured, leads to a sense of certainty and trust.*

Have you ever looked at other people and wished you could have the same strong, unwavering faith they have? Now is the time to realize that we all have that same capacity for faith.

One way to begin is to use the faith we do have, no matter how small or unsteady it may feel, because as we use it, it will increase, becoming stronger and stronger. In learning to swim, sooner or later we must take our foot off the bottom and begin moving through the water, or we will never learn to swim. The same holds true with faith and trust. We need to experiment with it, try it out and find out if it works. This process is the essence of faith and is the way in which it grows.

Put simply, to learn to trust it, test it!

When we do, we need to hold a positive attitude, for occasionally we may stumble and fall and experience a seeming 'failure'. If it happens, we need not be daunted and tempted to give up. Rather, we can be like an infant learning to walk—simply learn the lesson, get up and start again.

Prayer

Some people use prayer as an urgent and desperate plea for help at the eleventh hour when all else has failed. For others prayer is quiet meditation.

Some people regard prayer as muttering little memorized (or read) messages automatically, with little or no meaning for the one who is praying. Still others believe prayer is direct communion with God.

We say prayer is talking to God, communing with our innermost self. Meditation is listening out for God to talk to us.

In either case it is only a local call, not a long-distance one, and so we encourage everyone to do both regularly!

Fear, Faith and Prayer

As we suggest in Chapter Two, fear is one of our greatest enemies. It can hold us back from choosing to love. But unless we are willing to face our fears, we can never get rid of them. As long as we try to avoid our fears, they can become like monsters. When we have the courage to confront them, they begin to become more manageable, and sometimes even fade away into nothingness.

One way we can deal with fear is with faith and prayer. Faith is greater and more powerful than fear. We can affirm our faith and trust that all is well with the world, that a vast plan is unfolding, that all is in the hands of the Divinity Within, and that whatever is happening in our life is for the very best.

How to pray? To set the pace for the day, we can have a time of attunement in the early morning on awakening, before our mind becomes embroiled in all the events and activities of the day. Our life then is like a clean canvas without a mark on it. These first strokes upon waking need to be very clear and definite, full of love, inspiration and expectancy for the new day ahead.

We can tap into our innermost self and communicate with it. We can have faith that all our needs are being wonderfully met, even before we communicate them. This is where faith in our contact with the Divinity Within is so necessary. When we start the day in this way, we know it will be full of wonders because we are living in harmony with divine laws.

The guidance comes to each of us very clearly, if we but still ourself to hear it. Truth is simplicity itself, and therefore the smallest child can understand and follow it. God's ways may sometimes be very strange, but they are not complicated. Simplicity is the hallmark. If life ever becomes too complicated, it is of our own making.

We find that faith and prayer are something which need to be used and lived daily to be most effective in dealing with fear as well as our other concerns.

Inner Source of Wisdom

We have stated that trust (as everything else) must begin with ourself, that is, we must trust ourself before we are truly able to trust another. It means discovering and learning to trust our own inner source of wisdom.

At the Findhorn Foundation, whenever a need for information or a decision occurs, community members, after some thought and discussion let go of their own personal preference, close their eyes, take a few deep breaths and allow the required information to come to them from their inner source of wisdom. Surprisingly a consensus can often be reached quite quickly in this manner. It has been the principal method used by individuals and groups for making decisions in the community since it first began in 1962. Guidance from the God Within, or Inner Divinity is paramount.

This process is called *attunement,* for it enables us to attune to or connect with other aspects of ourself in addition to our cognitive mind, and then to allow whatever information or help we need to flow through this connection. We value attunement highly.

In attunement the form of response varies from person to person. It may come as images, words, sounds, feelings, a knowing or a sensing and in other ways as well. We need to experiment with it to discover in what form it operates for us.

For attunement to succeed, we need to be completely open, impartial and unattached to any specific outcome, or else we may distort or even block the process.

The key is to be completely relaxed and centred within ourself, so that we make a deep contact with our inner source of wisdom. Like most skills it may take some practice to increase our speed, clarity and accuracy, but if we stay with it, we shall discover countless applications for attunement.

EXERCISE: *Attunement*

Consider for a moment a current issue in your life relating to the theme of this book about which you would like to have more information—for example, how you can strengthen your faith and trust, or how you can deal effectively with your blocks to love.

Then consider whatever you have already done about it, if anything. Consider what you could do about it, the various options or alternatives you have and whatever you are actually ready and willing to do.

We suggest that you pre-record this exercise to enable you when you play it back to experience it freely and fully without interruption. Avoid rushing through it. Take your time.

Find a comfortable position, sitting up straight... Close your eyes ... Take several long, slow, deep breaths... Relax your body completely... Release all the tension... Allow whatever emotions you may be feeling to fade away... Do the same with your thoughts... Become like a calm, quiet lake, which mirrors perfectly the blue sky, or the starry sky in the silence of the night... Be at peace and yet remain alert...

Relax even more deeply... Count backwards slowly from ten to one, and on each succeeding number, feel yourself going farther and farther into the very centre of yourself... Feel yourself making a connection with your inner source of wisdom, that pure, permanent centre deep within you which has the answer to any question you could possibly ask about yourself...

When you are ready, silently ask your inner source of wisdom for the information or help you need about your issue, problem or concern... Take your time... Wait patiently in the silence, knowing something will soon come to you, knowing the help you seek is already on its way, perhaps in images, words, feelings or in other ways... Give it several minutes to emerge...

(Remain in the silence for as long as you wish.)

Then in your own time, allow everything to fade... Count slowly from one to ten, and on each succeeding number, feel yourself returning to your normal level of alert wakefulness... Bring your attention back to the room where you are now... Open your eyes... Take a deep breath... And a gentle stretch...

Make whatever notes or drawings you wish of your experience with this exercise. Has it given you any new insights or awareness?

Need for Discernment

Some people may question the appropriateness and validity of using attunement for information gathering, decision making and problem solving. They may ask, where is it coming from? How can I tell whether or not I am just making it all up in my mind? What about my instincts, wishes, fears and other feelings—can't they influence whatever prompting comes to me in the silence? How can I trust any of it?

These questions are all valid and important ones, and they indicate the need for judicious discernment and discrimination.

On one hand, whatever experience we have in the silence is worth exploring, as, like a dream, no matter what its source it can provide useful information about ourself. Obviously, a key issue is our proper interpretation and understanding of whatever comes to us. We suggest that you write everything down as a record, and then, if appropriate and you choose to do so, test it out, and note the results. As with faith, to strengthen and trust our attunement, we need to use it.

On the other hand, the source we contact at any one time in our attunement can be from various aspects of our *inner* life, including sensations, desires, emotions, thoughts, imaginings and intuitions, all valid and necessary psychological functions.

The source we contact can also come from *outer* influences. It is said we live in a psychic ocean, and many people receive extrasensory impressions in different ways from the environment around them.

Furthermore, the source can change from moment to moment, depending upon how quiet, clear and attuned we are able to remain.

Consequently, we suggest that you give yourself time to determine how valid an inner prompting may be before deciding to act upon it.

Until you have learned to discriminate as to the source of a prompting, do not allow yourself to be drawn into taking immediate action without first checking it. As with any skill, the development of attunement requires patience, persistence and practice.

Applying It

Improving Ourselves

Many of us are trying to improve ourselves, reading this and that literature, going to various lectures and workshops, studying under a master or teacher, or participating in this group or that community. These activities are signs we are searching for something. We are hungry for spiritual food.

We suggest that you find out which food—which spiritual path—is right for you, and then nourish yourself with it. Watch it grow and flourish within you. It all starts within you. By doing your own exploring, thinking, meditating and praying, you will be nourished. Your faith and trust will grow, and with it your ability to love.

Here are a few suggestions for developing faith and trust, and for strengthening direct communion with your inherent divinity.

1. Letter to God

Write a personal letter in which you express all you need to say to God. Include whatever feelings, thoughts, doubts, fears, resentments, judgements, questions, requests and appreciations are inside you and perhaps have been for a very long time. Hold nothing back. Express it all. Doing so helps to empty out the old to make room for the new.

2. Prayer

Prayer relaxes us into God's presence. If you have no method of prayer, try this simple one.

Find a quiet time and place. Every day set aside a definite period as your appointment with the Divinity Within—once, twice, as often as you can, but not so often that you will not keep it. Set aside a definite length of time—ten, twenty, thirty minutes, as long as you can, but not so long that you will not stay with it.

To begin your daily periods of prayer, become as still in your body as you can. Practice relaxing either sitting up straight or lying out flat. Stay relaxed and yet remain alert so you do not go to sleep.

Become as still in your mind as you can. Practice peaceful thinking. Realize every thought you think is a prayer, whether you are praying formally or not. Do not let your thoughts rule you. Rule your thoughts. Let no doubts, fears or other life-depleting thoughts enter in; if they do, deliberately fix your mind on positive, loving, constructive thoughts. Form them into affirmations. Repeat them over and over again, silently if you must, aloud if you can.

In your appointment with the Divinity Within, feel God's love, God's power. Feel God functioning in, through and for you. As you pray, bring God into every part of your life—your hopes and dreams, faults and failings, accomplishments and successes.

Pray for and with others. Keep a prayer journal and note for whom and what you pray; save space for noting results.

3. Dialogue with the Divinity Within

Create a symbolic representation of your Divinity Within and ask it specific questions. Wait patiently for the answers to come in one form or another, either right away or later during the day, or even after several days. Remember God is never in a hurry and yet is always on time!

Here is one way to do it. You may wish to pre-record this exercise to enable you when you play it back to experience it freely and fully without interruption. Avoid rushing through it. Take your time.

Close your eyes... Sit up straight ... Take a few deep breaths... Relax... Allow your body, emotions and thoughts to become still... Become like a calm, quiet lake...

When you are ready, allow to come to you an image or sense of your being in the room where you are now... In your imagination, see yourself sitting just the way you are... Begin to notice a very strong, very pure point of light glowing from within you... Let it become very clear, very definite and yet very soft, too...

This shining light is a symbol which represents your Divinity Within, the innermost part of yourself which loves you very much indeed... It is your Divinity Within, this radiant light within you, which fashions your life by creating all your lessons, your opportunities, your many blessings... It loves you... It protects you... It supports you... It guides you... It wants only the very best for you in every way...

Here is your opportunity to commune silently with your Divinity Within...
Express whatever feelings and thoughts you may have...
Ask whatever questions you may have ... Allow your Divinity Within
to respond in the silence... Take the next few moments to be with your
innermost self...

(Remain in the silence for as long as you wish.)

Know you can commune with your Divinity Within whenever you wish,
simply by choosing to go into the silence...

In your own time, allow everything to fade... Bring your attention back
to the room where you are now... Open your eyes... Take a deep breath...
And a gentle stretch...

Make whatever notes and drawings you wish of your experience with this exercise. Has it given you any new insights or awareness?

4. Writing an Autobiography

If you wish to deepen your self-awareness, self-understanding and self-acceptance, we recommend you write a comprehensive review and assessment of your life. Doing so sharpens your skills of self-observation and introspection, allows information to emerge from many levels of your being, and helps you to trace particular issues (such as trust) and make connections with various parts of your life. It also provides an excellent channel for creative self-expression.

Here are some hints for writing your life story.

Write it out in longhand. The act of writing itself helps to trigger ideas.

Use a loose-leaf notebook. It allows you to insert more material wherever you wish later.

Both authors find writing things out in longhand seems to forge a deeper inner contact, but if you are more used to using a digital device, then go right ahead and use it. Find whatever is comfortable for you.

Write about the events of your life in chronological order. It helps you to discover the origin and development of various traits, patterns and problems throughout your life.

Include a variety of events and issues about your:

- Childhood
- Education
- Health
- Leisure
- Relationships
- Sexuality
- Spirituality
- Thoughts and feelings
- Values and ideals
- Work

Take your time writing. Let your life's story be as long as you want it to be. Allow your writing to extend over weeks, months, even years if you wish. Welcome it as an exciting process of exploration and discovery, rather than as an ordeal to be completed as quickly as possible. Focus upon the journey, not the destination.

Suggested Reading

- *The Story of Your Life: Writing a Spiritual Autobiography,* by Dan Wakefield, offers a systematic approach to exploring our past and understanding our present. Through exercises such as drawing a favourite childhood room or describing a friend, we begin to understand the factors which help define our own spiritual journey.

Next in Chapter Four we explore how the qualities of honesty and openness relate to choosing to love.

4

Choosing to Be Honest and Open

In this chapter we examine the qualities of honesty and openness and the part they play in choosing to love.

Being True to Yourself

Two themes which run implicitly in our books are honesty and openness. We focus upon these qualities because they are absolutely essential for healthy and whole relationships. They are needed for clear communication. They lead to insight and understanding. They foster trust. When they are missing, either by ignorance or design, their absence blocks the free flow of love.

What Are Honesty and Openness?

Being honest is being truthful and authentic in word and deed, and therefore not devious, deceitful or false. Honesty reflects sincerity and integrity. Being honest is being candid, genuine and trustworthy.

Openness builds upon honesty. Being open is being unguarded, vulnerable, accessible to new ideas, and therefore not withholding, blocked or closed. Being open is being impartial, receptive and visible.

Most of us prefer to think of ourself as being honest and open. Yet sometimes we may withhold revealing the entire truth, tell 'little white lies', or become intentionally general, indirect or vague. Or we may practice 'relative' honesty, that is, varying with the person, the situation, the time, the place, the issue.

Being honest and open is being congruent, that is, presenting ourself on the outside consistent with who we are on the inside, and thus living our life as an open book.

Actually, we all are open books, no matter how much of ourself we may try to conceal. We all are as transparent as glass.

Do we not all receive intuitive impressions of each other? Do we not all see (or feel) past the words, past the actions, past the defences to the very heart, the very essence of one another? Do we not all (whether we know it or not) have a built-in radar which can penetrate the most elaborate defences? Can we not all usually tell when someone is being less than honest and straightforward with us?

Honesty and openness then are not a matter of revealing ourself to others, but of simply *confirming* to them what they may already see, feel and know. Rather than being instruments of strategy and defence, honesty and openness are a natural way of being, and accordingly make life much more simple, relaxed and fulfilling.

Personal Disclosure

One indicator of the limits of our honesty and openness is our attitude towards personal disclosure, that is, revealing information about ourself to others. For example, with whom and under what conditions are we willing to discuss honestly and openly details of our:

- Spiritual and religious beliefs

- Political views and affiliations

- Relationship history and challenges

- Age and date of birth

- Annual income and expenditures

- Sexual fantasies and practices

Or are they all taboo, and too personal, intimate and private to discuss with anyone else?

Another method is to consider those things we cannot joke about, make fun of or laugh over (either by ourself or with others)—those parts of life we regard as being too sensitive, serious, significant or sacred to be taken lightly.

These areas are worth exploring as limits to our openness, for if we hold these issues so carefully, where is the opportunity for flexibility, change, renewal, growth and development?

EXERCISE: *Reflective Meditation*

Rather than saying more about honesty and openness short exercises so that you may explore them directly rushing through them. Take your time, at least ten r one. You may wish to pre-record them.

The reflective meditation uses the cognitive mind t ity, symbol, seed thought or issue in all its meanings and implications. It explores and reflects upon the subject deeply and thoroughly. Good concentration is required to keep the mind focused, as well as persistence to probe deeply and discover new and relevant dimensions of the subject.

The reflective meditation is not simply taking stock or observing passively, but rather it aims at understanding, interpreting and evaluating whatever we discover within ourself. It results in a clear idea about the given subject and greater knowledge about ourself.

Close your eyes... Sit up straight... Take a few deep breaths...

Relax... Allow your body, emotions and thoughts to become still... Become like a calm, quiet lake...

When you are ready, begin to reflect upon the meaning of honesty and openness... Allow your mind to delve into them widely and deeply... Consider your experience of them, and all your feelings and thoughts about them... Address them from all angles... Contemplate them... Ponder them... Give your whole mind over to them...

Think about what honesty and openness are to you... Make notes for yourself as you do so...

When you have finished, examine your notes. What is the overall quality, tone or impression of your reflections? What similarities or patt~ you find? What are your feelings and thoughts about th

Make whatever notes or drawings you wi: this exercise. Has it given you any new insights

EXERCISE: *Receptive Meditation*

The preceding reflective meditation actively u However, in the receptive meditation, our attent the ordinary mind state and its awareness. It asks await an inner response to an issue from another part of ourself. An example of this form of meditation is asking for an image or other symbol to come into our awareness in response to a question, as we asked you to do in Chapter Two, *Finding a Symbol For Your Fear*.

An inner response or message is usually very brief, impersonal and meaningful. It may come in a variety of ways: a vision, intuition, inner hearing, words or even an urge to do something. It may also be experienced as a sense of inner contact with the Divinity Within.

We suggest that you always write down immediately whatever occurs to you during the meditation for better understanding and later reference. As you may have images or other symbols come to you, have drawing materials nearby.

Close your eyes... Sit up straight... Take a few deep breaths... Relax... Allow your body, emotions and thoughts to become still... Become like a calm, quiet lake...

When you are ready, use your imagination to picture or sense yourself putting into a bowl all the words, thoughts and feelings you considered about the qualities of honesty and openness in the reflective meditation...

Visualize placing the bowl above your head, and picture the sun shining brightly down upon it... Notice if any changes come about as a result of this action...

Then open yourself to receive images, words or other symbols which convey a deeper meaning of honesty and openness... Allow them to come to you... Do not think about it, or try to force anything to happen... Simply be receptive... Take your time... Take several minutes... Wait patiently in the silence for a deeper understanding of honesty and openness to come quietly to you... Let it emerge slowly...

(Remain in the silence for as long as you wish.)

In your own time, bring your attention back to the room where you are now... Open your eyes... Take a deep breath... And a gentle stretch.

Now create your own definitions of honesty and openness based upon experience in both the reflective meditation and the receptive tion.

Be aware that a relevant inspiration may come unexpectedly later, so do watch for it. For best results repeat these meditations daily on the same subject for at least seven days. Incidentally, we find that meditating with a group of people usually improves results with all three forms of meditation offered in this chapter.

Make whatever notes or drawings you wish of your experience with this exercise.

EXERCISE: *Creative (Ideal Model) Meditation*

The creative meditation may be used for a variety of purposes, chief among them *self-creation,* for with it we may transform aspects of our personality. It uses the creative power of thought, and it is to be repeated regularly until the desired results are obtained.

We use the creative meditation to do what is termed 'the inner work' of preparing ourself to take a step forward in our life. This method is based upon the psychological law which says that images or mental pictures and ideas tend to produce the physical conditions and the external acts which correspond to them. Put simply, every idea is a potential act in an initial stage. For more information about this law and others, refer to *The Act of Will,* Chapter Five, by Roberto Assagioli, MD.

Close your eyes... Sit up straight... Take a few deep breaths... Relax... Allow your body, emotions and thoughts to become still... Become like a calm, quiet lake...

Imagine how honest you would like to be, how truthful, sincere and authentic with yourself and others... Imagine how open you would like to be, how frank, unguarded and vulnerable... Let whatever you imagine be your free choice... Make certain you avoid all 'shoulds'...

It is not meant to be a model of perfection... But rather a realistic and attainable ideal... Something which would be possible to achieve during your life... Something you would be willing to be...

Then visualize yourself having these qualities fully available to you... Picture yourself as being this ideal model of yourself in relation to honesty and openness... How do you appear physically?...

How does your face appear?... Your eyes?... Your stance?... The rest of you?... What feelings and thoughts go with this ideal model?...

Next in your imagination, try on the ideal image like a coat... Identify with it... Merge with it... Become it... Be it... Experience what it would be like to embody this ideal model of yourself completely...

Then take a few minutes to visualize being in a number of everyday situations, possessing and acting out satisfactorily the qualities and attitudes of your ideal model... Bring your feelings into it as well...

Proceed through a typical day from morning to night and experience being this ideal... Include scenes in which you interact successfully in the various personal and professional roles you play, involving perhaps your parents... partners... family... friends... schoolmates or co-workers... and other people in your life... Take your time...

Make it as real and as vivid as possible...

(Remain in the silence for as long as you wish.)

In your own time, allow everything to fade... Bring your attention back to the room where you are now... Open your eyes... Take a deep breath... And a gentle stretch.

Make whatever notes and drawings you wish of your experience with this exercise.

Providing a Supportive Environment

We suggest that you repeat this exercise regularly until you feel the desired quality has firmly taken root and in your life. You may adapt this exercise to develop within yourself a wide variety of qualities, such as courage, joy, love, patience and peace. Refer to Chapter Six, *Transpersonal Qualities*.

Some people may question the long-term effect of this type of exercise. We would question it, too, if its purpose were simply to acquire a desired quality from *outside* ourself.

However, this exercise is based upon the principle that we have *within* ourself countless qualities, including the quality of love, which exist in potential, ready to be developed.

A relevant analogy is the acorn which carries within it all potential parts of a mighty oak tree: its root system, trunk, branches, leaves, even more acorns. To evoke the oak tree from the dormant acorn, we simply provide it with a supportive environment, including proper ongoing nourishment.

Our task therefore is not to wish or otherwise search outside ourself for more of whatever we want—courage, joy, love, patience, peace—but rather *to evoke from within ourself the seeds of the desired quality which are already there,* and then to provide a supportive environment, including proper ongoing nourishment, for them to grow and flourish.

Applying It

Here are a few suggestions for increasing your awareness of how honesty and openness function in your life.

1. Evening Review

One simple and effective method of exploring your attitudes and behaviour patterns regarding honesty and openness (and any other issues as well) is to set aside a few minutes each evening, ideally at bedtime, to review your day.

Take whatever time you have to give to it, whether a compressed two minutes or an expanded thirty minutes. However, avoid all pressure and stress. As with all of our self-help exercises, choose to do the evening review because you want to do it, and not because you feel you 'should' do it.

In your imagination replay the entire day as though it were on a film. Do it in reverse time. Begin with the present moment and review the events of the evening, then earlier in the afternoon and then finally in the morning, until you return to the moment you awakened.

Recall any face-to-face interactions, phone calls, written notes, texts and other electronic messages and letters.

Recall details of what and how you communicated with yourself and others, as well as what you may have held back, with whom and why.

Recall your actions (and inactions) and the statements they make about your relative honesty and openness.

It is most important that you conduct the evening review objectively as a detached observer, quietly witnessing the day's successes and 'failures' without being pulled back into them again and without judging either them or yourself. Simply gain dispassionately whatever awareness and insight you can from a given event, and then move on to the next one.

Writing down observations from an evening review is an added help in discovering more about attitudes and patterns of behaviour.

2. Messages and 'Shoulds' Scan

Find out how you were conditioned as a child regarding honesty and openness by reviewing your family history with these issues. Choose which aspects to keep and which to discard. Refer to Chapter Two, *Childhood Conditioning*.

3. Models of Behaviour

Choose three actual (not fictional) people you regard as good examples of honesty and openness. They may be from any time in history, or people you have known personally. Then use them as ideal models. Refer to Chapter One, *Models of Behaviour*.

Suggested Reading

- *Caring Enough to Confront,* by David Augsburger, says, "Truth and love are the two necessary ingredients for any relationship with integrity. Truth with love produces change and brings healing. Love me enough to tell me the truth."

- *Focusing,* by Eugene T. Gendlin, PhD, offers a self-help technique to resolve personal problems by perceiving specific steps of contact, felt change and deeper levels of awareness within our own physical body.

Next in Chapter Five we explore how our personal beliefs may block us from choosing to love.

5

Choosing to Be Aware

In this chapter we focus specifically upon our awareness, that is, how knowledgeable and understanding we are of our own experience and how it affects us.

What Is a Belief?

A belief is something we accept as being true for us, something we trust and have confidence in, usually based upon our personal conditioning and experience.

Are you aware of all you believe? Or do your beliefs operate automatically, without much thought, review or even deliberate choice on your part?

Are you aware of where each of your beliefs came from, that is, how and when they were formed?

Are you aware that you can change a belief—before it changes *you?* Or are beliefs chiselled into stone for you?

Many different beliefs may limit or block our bringing more love into our life. Therefore, for illustration, we take one common belief, trace its origin, examine its limiting effects and present techniques to deal with it.

Core Belief

At one time or another, most of us have doubts about ourself and our sense of worth. These doubts often come at a time when we feel we have made a mistake, done something we label wrong, stupid or bad, or seemingly 'failed' at something. Doubts may come when we feel judged or rejected or when we criticize ourself severely, even feel dislike or hatred for ourself.

If such doubts become habitual, they form a belief, such as, 'I am inadequate', 'I am not good enough', 'I do not deserve love', 'I cannot do anything right', or 'I am a failure'. Holding such beliefs usually results in a poor self-image, low self-worth and little or no self-confidence.

We call this doubt or fear about ourself a *core belief,* as it lies at the centre or core of our sense of self. It serves as a basic and very effective block to the full expression of our self-esteem, self-acceptance and self-love.

As this book suggests that we cannot love others until we first love ourself, it is important to examine our beliefs about ourself, particularly our self-worth. For example, what do you tell yourself at those times when you feel the least loving and accepting of yourself? What is your core belief about yourself?

EXERCISE: *Identifying a Core Belief*

Close your eyes... Sit up straight... Take a few deep breaths... Relax... Allow your body, emotions and thoughts to become still... Become like a calm, quiet lake...

When you are ready, allow yourself to experience the part of you which does not always like yourself very much... It may be the critic or judge inside of you... Take your time... Simply wait in the silence knowing it will come to you... Allow to come with it the thoughts and feelings, the doubts and fears this part of you has about your own self-worth... What does this part say to you?... What words does it use?... What is the worst thought, doubt or fear you have about your self-worth, your self-image?...

When you have found one or more of these thoughts or core beliefs about your self-worth, write them down.

Typical Operating Pattern

We find most people easily recognize and accept they have one or more of these core beliefs of low self-esteem. We have discovered a typical operating pattern: first someone in the environment triggers our core belief by saying or doing something which makes us feel inadequate; next we have an emotional reaction to whatever happened; and then we take some kind of compensatory action.

Core beliefs and their operating patterns are like an old-time music jukebox. When a button is pushed, the corresponding recording is selected, plays itself through, and then waits quietly until the next time the button is pushed, when it starts all over again. The same is true for an iTunes playlist.

A similar stimulus/response pattern involving our core belief continues equally automatically for a whole lifetime unless we take notice of it and choose to change it.

How do our buttons get pushed? Core beliefs may be activated in response to major life events, such as when we lose a job, our partner ends the relationship, or we otherwise 'fail' at some important task we set for ourself.

Our buttons are also triggered in a myriad of everyday events, such as when we feel unseen, unheard or misunderstood, or when we perceive ourself judged, ignored or rejected by others.

Our emotional reactions may vary from anger to anxiety, from despair to depression, from helplessness to hopelessness. Whatever form it takes, *our reaction results more from the core belief itself rather than from the immediate circumstances which trigger it* and, as such, is part of the jukebox/iTunes recording of our behaviour pattern.

Also part of the pattern are the compensatory actions we then take. We may turn to food, alcohol, drugs, sex, sleep, work, service or achievement. We may substitute money, prestige or professional recognition for the personal recognition and self-acceptance which elude us.

Some people experience their core belief constantly as an ever-present influence in their lives, while others seldom experience their core belief and its accompanying feelings of low self-worth. Rare is the person who has ever mastered completely this almost universal human pattern (no matter what they may tell themselves and others about having finished with it).

Self-Image and Validation

What causes a person to develop a poor self-image? One common explanation is that our self-image is the result of the validation we perceived from the significant people around us, especially during the first two years of life. For most of us, it means primarily our mother. Thus, if we felt recognized, accepted and nurtured by our mother during this period, then we undoubtedly felt good about ourself, and therefore developed a healthy self-image.

However, if we did not feel valued, we may have concluded it was our fault (something *was* wrong with *us)*, for otherwise, we would have been validated.

Harbouring this doubt about our worth in our infantile, two-year-old mind, we then began to look for further evidence to prove or disprove it.

As a result, over the years we amass substantial evidence to 'prove' that the core belief of low self-esteem we have about ourself is true. Thus, it becomes a perpetually self-fulfilling belief which, like the jukebox, repeats endlessly throughout our life unless we become aware of it and do something about it.

Notice this explanation does not suggest our parents failed to love us. They may have been simply ignorant or inept about making us feel welcomed and worthwhile, or we, ourself, may have had difficulty in recognizing or receiving their unique expressions of love.

In any case, we offer you the likely supposition that since we were about two years old, most of us have been re-creating regularly one basic scenario, complete with a whole cast of different characters, a variety of plots and circumstances, a range of emotional responses and a gamut of compensatory actions—all orchestrated to 'prove' the apparent 'truth' of our core belief of low self-esteem.

Limitation and Service Functions

As with all our behaviour patterns, the core belief limits us and it also serves us. On the one hand, it prevents us from experiencing our goodness, our wholeness; it blocks us from loving and accepting ourself and others.

On the other hand, our core belief also *gives* us something, it does something for us, or we would not allow it to continue to hold us back. For example, it may protect us, keep us safe, prevent us from taking risks, making mistakes or failing.

Recall from Chapter Two, *Functions of Fears,* one method to find out how any behaviour pattern (including our core belief of low self-esteem) serves us is to ask ourself what it is (1) we might lose and (2) we might have to *do* or *be* if it were *not* there as a part of us.

The 'bad' news is that most of us have a core belief of low self-esteem which hinders us from choosing to love.

The 'good' news is that we can do something about our core belief. We can minimize its powerful influence and limiting effects upon our life. We can prevent it from blocking us from loving ourself and others.

Taking Responsibility

As we suggest in Chapter Two, we have been conditioned by parents, family, social and political institutions and society at large. Such conditioning can be either desirable or undesirable, helpful or detrimental.

However, we need to take responsibility for our own attitudes and beliefs, no matter what their source may be or how we formed them.

Ken Keyes Jr. in his book *The Power of Unconditional Love* says, "You are not responsible for the programming you picked up in childhood. However, as an adult, you are 100 percent responsible for fixing it."

It is our explicit intention to help you to 'fix' whatever blocks you from bringing more love into your life.

Our Beliefs Determine Our Experience

While we accept our beliefs as being true for ourself, they may not be true for anyone else.

Ken Keyes Jr. also says, "A loving person lives in a loving world. A hostile person lives in a hostile world. Everyone you meet is your mirror." If we all live in the *same* world, how can that be?

It is because our beliefs are like tinted sunglasses through which we see the world; and the world as a mirror, reflects back to us whatever belief we present to it.

What kind of world do you see? A loving world? A hostile one? Or something else entirely different?

The kind of world we see and experience depends upon which glasses we wear, that is, it depends upon our beliefs—even though we may tell ourself it is the other way around.

Writer and educator Rue Wallace Hass sums it up clearly and concisely, 'What you see is who you are.'

So, what do you see? And who then are you?

It all depends upon the glasses you wear. It all depends upon your beliefs. You are what you believe.

Changing Beliefs

Are you willing to try on a new pair of glasses? Are you willing to consider updating your beliefs, perhaps even changing some of them?

It means taking a fresh approach. It means looking at things in a new way. For example, take a look at the illustration on the following page. What do you see?

Whatever you see, continue to explore the drawing. Look at it in a new way. Allow it to change and be something else, something different. What do you see now?

You may first see the silhouette of two individuals in profile facing each other. Or you may see a chalice or wine goblet.

Do you see both images? Keep looking at the figure until you find the chalice and the faces. To make our point, it is important you see both images.

When you find each of them, begin to switch your focus of attention back and forth several times between the faces and the chalice. Continue until you become aware of exactly *how* you manage to shift back and forth. What is the *inner* mechanism or process you use to cause your perspective to change instantly and totally from one image to the other?

For example, reminding ourself that both perspectives are present in the figure, we can simply command our awareness to shift from one image to the other. Our perspective can thus change with an act of will, that is, by our desiring and choosing for it to do so. Or perhaps you have used another method.

Re-Framing

Some people refer to this process as *re-framing,* taking a new look at something familiar to them, finding new perspectives, discovering new dimensions or exploring for new meanings and interpretations.

Notice the drawing itself does not change; it remains constant. Only our *perspective* changes by the way we interact with the drawing. Notice also that we cannot see *both* images at the same time.

Now imagine how it would be if we were to go through life only having seen *either* the chalice *or* the two faces. Imagine how it would be if we were to have a strong attachment to or personal investment in seeing only one of the images. Imagine how it would be if we were to fix upon that one image completely, thinking about it, reinforcing the image by holding tightly on to it in our awareness. Imagine how it would be if we were to be so convinced of the absolute certainty of the existence of only that one image that we become nearly incapable of seeing any other.

That is what can happen when we hold on to a belief rigidly. It is what can happen when we have looked through the same pair of sunglasses for so long we forget we are even wearing sunglasses.

Know Thyself

Most of us were conditioned as children not to talk about ourself and our sense of self-worth. Parents, teachers and others told us we would be considered impolite, ill-mannered, immodest, conceited, egotistical, even arrogant and narcissistic if we were to talk about our 'good points'. Discussing our strengths, telling others what we like about ourself or paying ourself a compliment are all usually frowned upon, if not altogether taboo, in most parts of Western society.

But accurate self-appraisal and self-appreciation are quite different from bragging and boasting.

The injunction 'Know thyself' surely means to recognize and accept both our strengths and our weaknesses, our positive qualities as well as our 'negative' ones, our assets as well as our liabilities, and to be able to talk about them simply, clearly and objectively.

EXERCISE: *Self-Appreciation*

Therefore, we invite you to begin to re-frame your self-image by considering for a moment everything you appreciate and love about yourself: habits, skills, qualities, traits, patterns, perspectives, feelings, ideas, ways of doing things.

NOTE. This is not to be a list of things you love *about life,* such as chocolate, dogs, roses, Mozart and the colour blue, but a list of what you love *about yourself.* Notice how you feel as you appreciate yourself. For example, do you feel warm and relaxed? Awkward and uneasy? Shy and embarrassed?

Close your eyes... Sit up straight... Take a few deep breaths... Relax...
Allow your body, emotions and thoughts to become stiff... Become like
a calm, quiet lake...

When you are ready, say aloud, 'What I love about myself is...' and
complete the sentence with a word or short phrase, whatever comes
spontaneously to you. Do not think about it. Then do it again, this time
allowing a new word or phrase to emerge. If you blank out momentarily,
simply begin again, knowing something will soon come to you.
Repeat it again and again for at least five to ten minutes. We suggest
that you keep a written record of your responses.

When you have finished, examine your responses, particularly the ones
which seem especially meaningful, significant or otherwise draw your
attention to them.

Make whatever notes and drawings you wish of your experience with
this exercise. Has it given you any new insight or awareness?

If you are a stranger to self-appreciation, find ways to introduce it into
your daily life. You owe it to yourself to recognize and acknowledge yourself in sincere and positive ways. As you do so, you will also be contradict-
ing your core belief of low self-esteem and re-framing your self-image.

To begin with, you may wish to keep your self-appreciations to yourself, but eventually you will need to begin to voice them aloud to others
('I appreciate the way I...' 'I am very good at ...' 'I love my own ...').

Otherwise you take part in a conspiracy of silence, a social convention
which limits you far more than it serves you.

Loyal Soldiers

In her book *The Unfolding Self: Psychosynthesis and Counseling* Molly
Young Brown introduces a useful analogy applicable to the core belief of
low self-esteem.

For years following the close of World War II, a Japanese soldier
would occasionally be discovered hiding in the jungle of a South Pacific
island. Unaware the war was over, he had kept himself alive, waiting to
be rescued. When found, he would be told he could stop hiding as the
war was over, but the disbelieving soldier would respond skeptically, "You
are trying to trick me." Eventually he would be subdued and repatriated
to Japan, where he would be retired from active duty with full military

honours as a hero for having served his country loyally, and would be re-integrated into civilian life.

We would like to offer the positive perspective that our core belief is a loyal soldier. It has served us well over the years. It has defended us. It has helped us to survive. It has kept us alive, perhaps through many battles and much pain.

But the war is over!

We have more options to protect ourself now than we did when we were two years old and first drafted our core belief into active duty. Out of hiding at last, our core belief need not be put to the firing squad for its limiting effects upon us, but rather be retired with full honours for having served us well. The time has come to transform and integrate it into our sense of wholeness.

As you begin to address it directly, do not be surprised if you encounter a 'You are trying to trick me' disbelieving resistance from the part of you which believes your core belief to be true. After all, it has been serving you for many years. But in time, with loving patience, you will be able to demonstrate clearly to it that for you the war is indeed finally over.

Applying It

Affirmations

Our brain is a computer. Our mind is the programmer. Our life is the printout. Most of us have been programming ourself with a core belief of low self-esteem from the time we were two years old. Our resultant printout has been doubt, hesitancy, poor self-image and lack of assurance, confidence, acceptance and love.

So, when we want to change the printout, what must we do? Yes of course, change the programming!

One effective means of changing the programming is with affirmations. *Affirmations are positive, seed-planting statements, images and actions which present clearly and precisely a desired outcome as if it were already achieved.* Used to overcome childhood conditioning, they are commands, given with authority, to our computer, our brain.

An example of a verbal affirmation from Chapter Two is *I always feel safe to choose to love.* An example of a visual affirmation is the Creative (Ideal Model) Meditation of honesty and openness in Chapter Four. An example of an action affirmation is the 'Acting As If' technique described later in this chapter.

People may ask how repeatedly saying a sentence, visualizing an image or effecting physical postures and movements can change a life-long behaviour pattern. Affirmations are a means of switching our focus of attention similar to the way we switch our focus from one image to the other in the chalice/faces drawing. They are a means of changing our *perspective* about ourself. They are a new pair of glasses we offer ourself—a new positive belief.

Affirmations are used to re-frame a given situation, in this case, our self-esteem. They are based on the psychological law which says that attention, affirmation and repetition reinforce the ideas and images on which they are centred. For more information about this law refer to *The Act of Will,* Chapter 5, by Roberto Assagioli, MD.

We present the following three affirmation techniques to help you to re-frame your core belief of low self-esteem and to begin to love and accept yourself more fully.

1. Verbal Affirmations

Effective verbal affirmations have these characteristics:

- They are stated positively and vigorously. (*'I am always very confident now'*, rather than 'I am no longer fearful'.) They focus upon the new attitude we wish to create, rather than the old one we want to let go.

- They are short, usually a dozen words or less. Most core beliefs of low self-esteem are equally short ('I am inadequate', 'I am not good enough', 'I cannot do anything right', 'I am a failure'), and notice how effective they have been all our lives!

- They are stated in present tense, as if the desired outcome has already been achieved. (*'I always feel very safe to be open to love now'*, rather than 'I will feel increasingly safe to be open to love in the future'.)

- They begin with our name to keep them personal and connected to our own developing process. (*'I, (Name), always deserve love in my life.'*)

- They are absolute. Using words such as *always, very* and *now* and avoiding phrases such as *I can, I try to,* or *I have the ability to,* helps to close loopholes so the part of ourself which believes our core belief to be true can find no room for exceptions.

- They are limited to ourself and our own life because we cannot make affirmations on behalf of other people. (*'I am always very loving and lovable'*, rather than 'People always find me very loving and lovable'.)

- They are enhanced when we visualize the desired outcome as we write the affirmations and say them aloud.

The difference between an affirmation and a core belief is the core belief is a lie which seems like the truth. An affirmation is the truth which seems like a lie!

To create a verbal affirmation which reverses or contradicts the core belief of low self-esteem may be simply to state the opposite. For example, if our core belief is 'I am not good enough', our affirmation might be *'I am always good enough'*, or *'I am absolutely perfect just as I am now'*. Make it seem like the biggest lie you could possibly tell. It will be a stronger, more effective affirmation if you do!

Say it several times, beginning with, *'I, (Name), ... '* Each time visualize the desired outcome to reinforce the re-programming of your computer, the re-framing of your self-esteem. Take your time. Keep it fresh, energetic and alive.

Here are some suggestions for reinforcing your affirmation:

- Say it occasionally as you make eye contact with yourself in a mirror.

- Write it down over and over again, visualizing the desired outcome as you do so.

- Write it on index cards, then put them up around your home or work place.

- Carry an index card with you in your pocket, wallet or purse as a daily reminder.

- Go public with it. Telephone/text friends and say/write it confidently to them.

- Find a picture or make a drawing which symbolizes whatever you wish to achieve, display it prominently and hold it clearly in your awareness.

Continue to look for new and novel ways to remind yourself of your affirmation. Keep it a living presence in your day-to-day life. Remember, you are re-framing. You are re-programming your computer. Most importantly, *you* are the one who is creating the outcome you desire.

Almost all advertising influences us by using affirmations in a strategy of frequent repetition over a period of time. We can use the same strategy. We suggest that you avoid feelings of impatience and hurry to give your affirmation the time it needs to take root. Repetition is the key. The original programming you wish to change did not develop overnight; neither is it likely to disappear overnight. With affirmations, as with advertising, persistence produces results.

2. Visual Affirmations

A graphic form of affirmation is the Creative (Ideal Model) Meditation in which we picture and experience in our imagination specific details of how we would like our life to be.

Now turn back to Chapter Four, and review your experience of the Creative Meditation. Then re-play the ideal model technique in your imagination, substituting the quality of love for the qualities of honesty and openness you used originally, and visualizing and experiencing how loving you would ideally like to be. Thus, you give both your conscious and unconscious mind a simple and clear blueprint to follow.

3. Action ('Acting As If') Affirmations

A third affirmation technique is the reverse of the first two: it uses outer behaviour to produce a change in our inner state. With sufficient repetition over a period of time, we can actually change our inner state to match the outer behaviour we enact. We do it by 'acting as if' we already possessed the desired inner state.

People commonly use this technique in everyday life. For example, we know we can change how we are feeling by such simple outer actions as singing or whistling, or by the way we dress, or by the way we speak, stand and move. The outer action is the catalyst for the inner change.

By behaving as if we were feeling cheerful, confident, courageous or loving, eventually we become that which we enact. Students of Psychosynthesis will recognize the sound psychological law behind this technique which states that attitudes, movements and actions tend to evoke corresponding images and ideas.

First consider outer, observable behaviour which reflects the quality of love to you. Begin with physical sensations, postures, gestures, movements and actions you can enact privately, preferably while facing a large mirror. Apply them all towards yourself, 'acting as if' you loved and accepted yourself genuinely and fully, and you possessed a high level of self-confidence and self-esteem.

Later when you are comfortable with this technique, begin to identify specific outer, observable actions you can take when you are relating to others, 'acting as if' you loved them freely and fully, even (and especially) if you are feeling quite the contrary towards them at the time.

NOTE. By 'acting as if' we feel love for ourself or others when we may actually feel quite negative emotions, we are not being deceitful, hypocritical or inauthentic, *if* our intention is to identify with and evoke the innermost, purest level of ourself *despite* our 'negative' or blocked feelings. While it is necessary for us to accept all parts of ourself, we do have the *choice* of which conflicting parts to energize and express—the positive or the 'negative', the highest or the lowest, the loving or the unloving. This important choice is *always* ours to make.

Suggested Reading

- *Vivation,* by Jim Leonard and Phil Laut, says that "once you accept the idea that your reality is a projection of your mind, you begin to eliminate the tendency to feel like a victim and the desire to prove yourself right about your negative convictions. Accepting that your reality is the projection of your mind is giving yourself the opportunity to create for yourself the things you want in life."

- *I Deserve Love,* by Sondra Ray, shows how to use affirmations and presents hundreds of sample affirmations tailored for use in many different loving and sexual situations.

Next in Chapter Six we explore how recognizing and accepting *all* parts of ourself is an important step in choosing to love.

6
‒

Choosing to Accept

In this chapter we examine our personal identity as being a composite of the many different images we have of ourself and that accepting them all is an important step in choosing to love.

What Is Acceptance?

The chapter title *Choosing To Accept* means accepting ourself as we are – accepting *all* parts of ourself – without judgement, criticism or condemnation. It is also accepting others as they are without wanting them to be any different than they are.

Acceptance is not denial, tolerance or resignation. We can certainly change the parts of ourself we wish to improve, but only *after* we accept them.

Otherwise the parts of ourself we do not recognize and accept, both our positive qualities and our 'negative' ones, we tend to project onto others; and therefore, we do not see others as they are, we see only our projections.

Consequently, as we are more able to accept ourself, we are more able to see and accept other people more clearly and genuinely. Thus, accepting all parts of ourself is a necessary step towards loving freely and fully.

Self-Images

We all have many different parts. We can call them images or identifications that we have of ourself. However, each one is only a fragment, a partial image, because we are always changing and expressing different ones at different times. Each image we have of ourself then is only one composite piece of our total personal identity.

We have countless other pieces, other images—so many that it would be impossible to list them all. For example, most of us can honestly say:

'Sometimes I Am a...'

Achiever	Egotist	Optimist
Activist	Enemy	Organizer
Addict	Entertainer	Outsider
Adolescent	Exaggerator	Pacifist
Adult	Extrovert	Parasite
Adversary	Failure	Perfectionist
Advisor	Fanatic	Pessimist
Ally	Fighter	Pragmatist
Angel	Fixer	Procrastinator
Appreciator	Follower	Realist
Athlete	Fool	Rebel
Baby	Friend	Receiver
Beggar	Giver	Romantic
Bigot	God	Saboteur
Bitch	Gossip	Sage
Bore	Helper	Saint
Catalyst	Idealist	Sceptic
Cheat	Innovator	Sinner
Clown	Insider	Spy
Comforter	Introvert	Student
Communicator	Joker	Success
Competitor	Judge	Supporter
Complainer	Leader	Teacher
Consumer	Listener	Thief
Controller	Loser	Tourist
Creator	Lover	Tramp
Critic	Magician	Tyrant
Cynic	Manipulator	Victim
Deceiver	Monster	Villain
Defender	Mystic	Wallflower
Destroyer	Nuisance	Winner
Devil	Observer	Worrier
Dreamer	Opponent	Zealot

In addition there are many other images we have of ourself at one time or another. A few of the more obvious ones relate to our:

- Gender
- Family
- Nationality
- Political persuasion
- Home responsibilities
- Work
- Religious/spiritual persuasion
- Hobbies and pastimes
- Attitudes, beliefs, desires
- Physical body/sensations
- Emotions and feelings
- Mind and mental processes

This brief survey represents a very small fraction of a rich, ever-changing mosaic comprising our personal identity. It only hints at a colourful cast of characters we carry within us waiting to be accepted and integrated within our sense of self.

Identification

One powerful Psychosynthesis method which aids self-acceptance is known as Identification. It invites us to explore various parts of ourself directly and fully. It entails facing them squarely, examining them freely from all sides and accepting them completely as a part of ourself. Identification is one part of a two-part process. We present the other part in Chapter Seven.

Identification takes several forms. One common form has five steps. The first step asks us to visualize a relevant need, desire, trait or attitude in symbolic form, such as a person, animal or object. The second step then asks us to explore the symbol for whatever qualities it expresses to us. The third step invites us to make a drawing of the symbol as a means of anchoring it within our awareness.

The fourth step calls for us to interact and dialogue with the symbol to learn more about the part of us it represents. The final step asks us to become the symbol, that is, to imagine ourself as actually being the symbol, identifying with it completely, to gain insights about how this part of us feels, thinks and behaves—that is, how *we* feel, think and behave when we are expressing this part of ourself.

EXERCISE: *Personal Identification*

To experience Identification for yourself, select a personal image or identity you would like to find out more about, perhaps one from the above listings. You may wish to pre-record this exercise, on a digital device of your choice for ease of use. Avoid rushing through it. Take your time.

> *Close your eyes... Sit up straight... Take a few deep breaths... Relax... Allow your body, emotions and thoughts to become still... Become like a calm, quiet lake...*
>
> *When you are ready, allow to come into your awareness an image or other symbol which represents the personal identity you have selected ... Take your time... Wait patiently in the silence, knowing something will soon come to you which represents this personal identity ...*
> *Be willing to accept whatever comes without judging, censoring or rejecting it ... Simply be ready to observe and examine it, with the purpose of learning more about it ...*
>
> *As you begin to sense something, allow it to become more vivid ...*
> *Note its size and shape... Its density and design... Its colour and texture... Explore it with as many of your senses as you can ...*
> *Find the overall quality it suggests to you...*

Then open your eyes, and express in words or a drawing either the image itself or its quality... If nothing has come to you, hold the question in mind and begin to write or draw freely and spontaneously, letting something come to you in that way...

Note the overall *quality* of the symbol and any other words, feelings or thoughts which came to you during the exercise, or you are aware of now.

We continue with the fourth and fifth stages of the exercise.

> *Close your eyes... Become like a calm, quiet lake again...*
> *When you are ready, allow the image or other symbol of your personal identity to return to you... No matter what it is, treat it as a Walt*

71

Disney character having the capacity to talk with you ... As when you encounter a stranger on a train or airplane, your symbol may or may not be very friendly, cooperative or communicative ... Remain as detached and objective as possible, give it the freedom to be itself and learn whatever you can... It is all right if it seems you are making it up in your imagination...

Find out as much as possible about it ... Its history... How long it has been a part of you... What it needs... How it serves you ... How it limits you... How you might deal with it ... Take your time... Spend several minutes interacting with it ... Learn all you can... Do it now before continuing with the following instructions ...

(Continue to dialogue with the symbol for a few moments.)

Then in your imagination, try on this symbol like a coat... Step into it ... Merge with it ... Become it ... Feel what it is like to be this symbol completely... As this symbol, what are your feelings?... What are your thoughts?... What are your needs?... What are your motivations?... Take your time to explore this part of yourself from its own point of view...

(Continue to identify as the symbol for as long as you wish.)

When you are ready, allow yourself to separate from this symbol ... Step back and away from it ... Return your awareness and attention to yourself once again... And resume the dialogue with the symbol as before ...

(Continue to dialogue with the symbol for as long as you wish.)

When your dialogue has come to an end, in your own time allow everything to fade... Bring your attention back to the room where you are now... Open your eyes... Take a deep breath... And a gentle stretch...

Write down any feelings, thoughts and questions you wish to record from your identification with your personal identity. Note especially how it serves you, how it limits you and whatever it says it needs.

Subpersonalities

Another Identification technique invites us to imagine an image or identity we have of ourself as being a separate person, with its own name, personality, feelings, thoughts and behaviour. We call it a subpersonality, as it is only a part of our personality, not the whole of it. It is only one of our inner cast of characters.

Each subpersonality has its own unique expression. For example, whenever we are feeling helpless and victimized (and therefore expressing our 'Victim' subpersonality), we stand, sit, feel, think, move, talk and act differently than we do whenever we are feeling, say, assertive, strong and powerful (perhaps expressing a 'Leader' subpersonality).

Subpersonalities may be likened to musicians in an orchestra. They each have their part to play and their contribution to make to the whole. For many people, however, it is an orchestra without a conductor, and so most of the musicians consider themselves to be star soloists, have their own music to perform and take the spotlight away from all the others whenever they can.

Conflicts

Conflicts abound. Rather than all playing the same music and blending harmoniously together, they sound collectively more like the pre-concert tune-up. They are undisciplined and uncoordinated. They need a leader, someone to take charge, directing and harmonizing their talents and all they have to offer to the whole.

In the same way, parts of ourself compete for attention and expression. When we experience ambivalence, indecision or conflict within ourself, we can say that two or more of our subpersonalities are in disagreement. For example, one part of us wants to be in a committed loving relationship, while another part wants freedom and independence above all else.

A common conflict for many people occurs between our 'Mystic' subpersonality and our 'Pragmatist'. Our 'Mystic' part says, "All you need to do in life is to put your faith and trust in God, set all your worries aside and go with the flow. You can always depend on God to provide for all your needs and to take good care of you."

Our 'Pragmatist' counters with, "Nonsense! You can't pray your troubles and responsibilities away and leave everything for God to do. Besides God doesn't have to pay the rent or put food on the table. *I* am the one who has to do it!"

Our 'Sceptic' subpersonality may suddenly appear, declaring, "What makes you two so sure there even is a God?" Within no time, we may have constellations of other subpersonalities joining forces and taking sides in the debate, leaving our internal state in utter conflict, confusion and ambivalence. With no obvious conductor on the scene, the orchestra falls quickly into chaos.

Clearly, we need a leader to resolve such conflicts and to harmonize and coalesce all the many parts of ourself. The discovery of our leader is the subject of Chapter Seven, and the employment of our leader is outlined in Chapter Eight.

Transpersonal Qualities

The Divinity Within draws upon many transpersonal qualities or universal principles which it seeks to express through us. The *Angel Meditation Cards*, developed at the Findhorn Foundation as a part of the *Game of Transformation*, depict a few of these archetypal qualities. There are many others of course, but this list gives a sense of the many pure qualities which are standing by, waiting for people to experience and express.

- Abundance
- Adventure
- Balance
- Beauty
- Birth
- Brotherhood
- Clarity
- Communication
- Compassion
- Courage
- Creativity
- Delight
- Education
- Efficiency
- Enthusiasm
- Expansion
- Expectancy
- Faith
- Flexibility

- Forgiveness
- Freedom
- Grace
- Gratitude
- Harmony
- Healing
- Honesty
- Humour
- Inspiration
- Integrity
- Joy
- Light
- Love
- Obedience
- Openness
- Patience
- Peace
- Play
- Power

- Purification
- Purpose
- Release
- Responsibility
- Risk
- Simplicity
- Spontaneity
- Strength
- Surrender
- Synthesis
- Tenderness
- Transformation
- Trust
- Truth
- Understanding
- Vision
- Willingness

Such a quality lies at the core of each subpersonality, whatever its outer behaviour may be. For example, an aggressive 'Bully' subpersonality may have at its core the quality of Power. A 'Judge' subpersonality may have at its core the quality of Discernment. A 'Sentimentalist' subpersonality may have at its core the quality of Love. Thus, all subpersonalities may be regarded as *distortions* of these pure qualities which are hidden gifts waiting to be found and claimed.

Therefore, if we try to eliminate a seemingly 'undesirable' aspect or subpersonality from our behaviour (for example the part of us who judges), we actually deprive ourself of the real gift it has to offer us. The challenge is to recover the gift by making the best use of our subpersonality and enabling it to express itself in a more coordinated, positive, helpful way. As we recognize, accept and express a subpersonality, and claim the gift at its core, it becomes more integrated into the whole of us, rather than remaining a disconcerting, disconnected fragment.

Referring to drives, urges, needs and other distinctive forms of personal behaviour as subpersonalities helps us to:

- Form them and give them structure
- Bring them more clearly into our awareness
- Deal with them constructively and systematically
- Reclaim and express positive parts of ourself

Our task is not the negative one of judging and making any part of ourself 'wrong' or 'bad', and subsequently trying to dispose of it. Rather it is the positive task of reforming and harmonizing it with other parts of ourself, and therefore activating the positive quality it brings to our life. This process starts with recognizing and accepting the subpersonality completely, embracing it fully as it is, without judgement, criticism or embarrassment. As we learn to accept all parts of ourself, we are more able to accept all parts of others, a vital step in loving ourself and others unconditionally.

EXERCISE: *Meeting a Subpersonality*

In Chapter Two you identified a specific fear which stops you from bringing more love into your life. In Chapter Five you identified a core belief of low self-esteem which may seriously limit your giving and receiving love fully. We now invite you to meet the part of you which blocks you from bringing more love into your life.

Here is an extended exercise. We suggest that you pre-record it. Avoid rushing through it. Take your time. Give yourself at least 30 minutes for this exercise. First consider for a moment the part of yourself which blocks you from bringing more love into your life. Consider how you experience it in your life.

Close your eyes... Take a few deep breaths... Relax... Allow your body, emotions and thoughts to become still... Become like a calm, quiet lake...

When you are ready, imagine being out in the countryside, in the middle of a beautiful meadow... It is a warm, pleasant day ... Feel the ground under your feet... Feel the warmth of the sun shining down upon your body... See the blue sky, the trees, grass and other plants... Hear the sounds of nature around you ... Smell the fresh fragrance of the countryside... Experience the peace and contentment here...

After a while, you notice that at the far side of the meadow is a house, and you are standing upon a footpath which leads directly to it ... You decide to examine the house more closely, and so you begin walking towards it ...

As you come nearer to the house, you see a sign which says, 'The House of My Subpersonalities'... You hear sounds coming from the house as you begin to walk around it, first along one side, then along the rear of the house, then along the other side, until at last you come once again to the front of the house...

You walk up to the front door, knock upon it, and call through the door into the house, asking the subpersonality who represents the part of yourself which blocks you from bringing more love into your life to come outside to talk with you... Then move back a few steps, and wait...

A moment later, the door opens, and out comes the subpersonality who represents the part of yourself you wish to explore...

What does it look like—what is its appearance?... Try not to judge, censor or reject it ... Simply observe and examine it with the purpose of learning more about it ...

Treat your subpersonality, no matter what it is, as a Walt Disney character having the capacity to talk with you, and begin to dialogue with it ...

Find out as much as possible... Its name... Its history... Its needs... Its underlying motivation—why it does the things it does... How it serves you... How it limits you... The positive transpersonal quality at its core it offers to you... Take your time... Spend several minutes interacting with it ... Learn all you can... Write down the main points as they emerge...

(Continue to dialogue with the subpersonality for a few moments.)

Then, in your imagination, try on this subpersonality like a coat ... Step into it ... Merge with it ... Become it ... Feel what it is like to be this subpersonality completely... As this subpersonality, what are your feelings?... What are your thoughts?... What are your needs?... What are your motivations?... Take your time to explore this part of yourself from its own point of view...

(Continue to identify as the subpersonality for as long as you wish.)

When you are ready, allow yourself to separate from this subpersonality... Step back and away from it ... Return your awareness and attention to yourself once again... And resume the dialogue with the subpersonality as before...

(Continue to dialogue with the subpersonality for as long as you wish.)

When your dialogue has come to an end, in your imagination, sense a beam or column of sunlight shining down upon you and your subpersonality, filling and enfolding you both within its light and warmth... Notice if any changes appear in either of you...

You become aware that the column of light is actually a radiant lift or elevator, and that you and your subpersonality, standing within it, begin to rise slowly upwards... You feel perfectly comfortable, calm and safe, as though it were a normal, everyday occurrence... You continue to ascend, and the ground begins to fall faster away from you...

Soon you can see not only the whole house clearly, but all the meadow... Higher and higher the two of you rise within the column of light until the entire countryside becomes a vast magnificent panorama, stretching out before you in all directions as far as you can see...

Now you begin to enter a bank of fleecy white clouds... Soon all the earth below fades from view, as you become completely enveloped by the clouds...

*A moment later you rise above the clouds and witness an amazing sight:
a beautiful, immaculate garden with grass, bushes, trees and many
different kinds of flowers... All the blossoms everywhere are a dazzling
white... It is a place of safety, love and support... As you step from the
column of light onto a neatly-trimmed garden path, you feel total peace
and contentment...*

*After a while, you see coming towards you a wise and loving guide,
someone who knows and loves you very much indeed, and with whom
you feel quite safe and completely at ease... The guide says to you, "I am
here to help you. Speak with me about the concerns you have. I know all
about you, and I am able and willing to answer any question you may
have about yourself and your subpersonalities."*

*Begin to talk with this wise and loving guide about your subpersonality
for the next several minutes... Allow all three of you to ask and answer
questions for each other and to discuss mutual concerns... Discuss what
your subpersonality needs and how best to deal with it ... Write down the
main points as they emerge...*

**(Continue to dialogue with the guide and the subpersonality for as
long as you wish.)**

*When the dialogue has finished, the guide gives you a tangible gift to help
you deal with this subpersonality, perhaps a symbolic reminder of some
kind, and says to you, "Know that you may return to this white garden as
often as you wish and speak with me about any concern you may have.
I am here to help you. As you have discovered, I know all about you, and
am able and willing to answer any question you could possibly ask about
yourself."*

*You thank the guide for the gift and say goodbye... You return with your
subpersonality to the column of light... The two of you enter it once
again and begin to descend slowly and safely... Soon you enter the bank
of clouds, and the beautiful white garden fades from view...*

*A moment later you emerge below the clouds where you see the familiar
countryside stretching out before you... As you continue to descend, the
ground comes up to greet you... In only a few moments, you and your
subpersonality stand firmly upon the ground again, near the front door
of the house in the meadow... Notice if any changes appear in either one
of you...*

You ask your subpersonality if it has anything more to say to you, any final questions, comments... You say anything you need to say to it too...

Then you say goodbye to your subpersonality and allow it to go back inside the house... Be aware that you may return to this house any time you choose, and talk with this subpersonality or any other one you desire...

You begin to walk along the footpath which leads into the meadow to where you first began... As you do, feel the ground under your feet...

Feel the warmth of the sun shining down upon your body... See the blue sky, the trees, grass and other plants ... Hear the sounds of nature around you... Smell the fresh fragrance of the countryside... Experience the peace and contentment here...

In your own time, allow everything to fade... Bring your attention back to the room where you are now... Open your eyes... Take a deep breath... And a gentle stretch...

Write down any feelings, thoughts and questions you wish to record from this visualization. Include the token gift which the guide may have given you to deal with this particular subpersonality.

To complete the exercise, close your eyes again... Become like a calm, quiet lake...

When you are ready, allow to come into your awareness the positive transpersonal quality this subpersonality offers to you... How often do you experience this quality presently in your life?...

Which part of yourself stops you from having more of this quality?... How?... Why?...

Imagine how it would be to have more of this quality in your life... What would life be like then?... What would be different?... How would your relationships be?...

Would you like to have more of this quality in your life?... If so, how might you begin to do it?... What 'next step' are you willing to take?...

Visualize and experience yourself taking this step successfully and having more of this quality in your life...

Then in your own time, allow everything to fade... Bring your attention back to the room where you are now... Open your eyes... Take a deep breath... And a gentle stretch...

Make whatever notes or drawings you wish of your experience with this exercise. Has it given you any new insights or awareness?

In summary, the method of Identification shows that we always need to be willing to re-define ourself, finding, accepting and expressing new parts, insights and dimensions of our personal identity, rather than considering ourself as a set package of fixed proportions.

Applying It

How many subpersonalities is it possible to have? The psychologist Gordon Allport states that the English language has some 18,000 designations for distinctive forms of personal behaviour; this figure is multiplied greatly when they appear in combination! So, we have virtually an unlimited number of subpersonalities to draw upon to express our own uniqueness.

The Technique of Subpersonalities

Here are a few suggestions for using the technique of subpersonalities.

1. Morning Preview

Each morning consider which of your subpersonalities might be useful for you to identify with and express at certain times or places during the day. Then remember to do it.

2. Identification

Say to yourself regularly, *'Who* (what part of me—which subpersonality) is experiencing and reacting to this person or situation now?' Also, be aware of which of your subpersonalities is speaking whenever you use the word 'I'.

3. Subpersonality Creative Visualization

Use subpersonalities to deal with other subpersonalities. For example, go to the house in the meadow and ask to dialogue with the subpersonality who can best help you to deal with a problem subpersonality.

4. Evening Review

Each evening, review your day to find which subpersonalities were most active and in what specific circumstances. Also review the past to find out when a given subpersonality has been active. Look for repeating patterns.

Suggested Reading

- *Subpersonalities: The People Inside Us,* by John Rowan, is a comprehensive book for people interested in their personality and how it helps or hinders their everyday life. It traces the origins, development, functions, uses and potentials of subpersonalities, and is addressed to psychologists and lay readers alike.

Next in Chapter Seven we meet the conductor of the orchestra comprising all our subpersonalities.

7

Choosing to Be Free

In this chapter we search for the real you.

Who Are You?

Who are you? Who is underneath all the images, identifications and roles? Where is the conductor of your orchestra of subpersonalities? These questions and their answers form the basis of Chapter Seven.

As we have seen in Chapter Six, we experience ourself in different ways at different times. However, we tend to identify ourself *primarily* in one of the following five ways:

1. I Am My Body

I am very in touch with my body and its physical sensations. It gives me the solid sense of being alive. I and my body are one. I live in an outer, physical world, and I contact and embrace life mostly through my body. The real me would not exist without it. My body is basically who I am.

2. I Am My Emotions

I am very sensitive to my emotions, and I feel them intensely. They make me feel alive. I and my emotions are one. I live in a passionate, affective world, and I perceive life mostly through my emotions. The real me would not exist without them. My emotions are basically who I am.

3. I Am My Desires

I am very motivated by my drives. They empower me and give me a satisfying sense of being alive. I and my desires are one. I live in a spontaneous and ever-changing world of human drives and impulses, and I experience life mostly through trying to satisfy my desires. The real me would not exist without them. My desires are basically who I am.

4. I Am My Mind

I know I am very attuned to my mind and its thoughts and ideas, and I think that the intellect, knowledge and understanding are very important. They let me know I am alive. I and my mind are one. I live in a rational, cognitive world, and I am aware of life mostly through my mind. The real me would not exist without it. My mind is basically who I am.

5. I Am My Roles

I am very engaged in many activities and portray many different roles, such as son or daughter, mother or father, wife or husband, teacher or student, artist or executive. They affirm my being alive. I and my roles are one. I live in a multifaceted world and play many parts which I perform for the benefit of myself and others. I experience life mostly through my roles. The real me would not exist without them. My roles are basically who I am.

Which of these descriptions do you identify with primarily?

Identification

In Chapter Six we say the method of *Identification leads us to step into the partial image,* take it on, become it and express it to learn more about it, recognize it, accept it and express it and the gifts it offers more effectively. It is one stage of a two-stage process.

All these images are not only partial ones, but they can change, and therefore they are not basically *who* we are, because our essential Divinity Within is always the same—pure, permanent and unchanging. From infancy to adulthood to end of life as we know it, this one place within ourself is constant, always remaining the same.

It is the detached, impartial observer within us who has been aware of everything we have ever experienced throughout our entire life. It is this innermost place within ourself which Psychosynthesis calls our Personal Self.

Disidentification

Here in Chapter Seven we explore the other stage of the process. Once we have fully acknowledged and identified with a part of ourself (and not until then), the Psychosynthesis method of *Disidentification leads us to step back from the partial image,* disconnect from it, move some distance away from it—not to deny, avoid, suppress or stop it, but rather to observe it, gain greater perspective on it and, if we have not already done so, to recognize it, accept it and harmonize it more effectively with other parts of ourself.

One way for us to experience this permanent centre within ourself, then, is to take one step back from everything we identify with so that we can experience who we are when we are not being all these other things.

The task is to peel off *all the* partial images we have of ourself like so many layers of an onion to reveal our centre, the permanent place within us which does not change. To find out who we are, we simply remove temporarily all who we are *not,* that is, all our partial images and identifications, all our various subpersonalities and roles.

EXERCISE: *Self-Awareness*

This exercise formulated originally by Roberto Assagioli, MD, helps us to step back in order to experience who we essentially are. It is in two sections. The first is the peeling-off part and helps us to examine the partial images of ourself while maintaining the point of view of the observer, recognizing *the observer is not that which he or she observes.* It then leads us to the second section in which we become aware of our centre, our Personal Self or 'I'.

We suggest that you pre-record this exercise, on any device you are comfortable with using. Avoid rushing through it. Take your time.

> *Close your eyes... Sit up straight... Take a few deep breaths ... Relax...*
> *Allow your body, emotions and thoughts to become still... Become like a*
> *calm, quiet lake...*
>
> *When you are ready, affirm the following statements slowly to yourself...*

Section One

> *I have a body and physical sensations, but I am more than my body and*
> *physical sensations... My body may find itself in different conditions of*
> *health or sickness, it may be rested or tired, but that has nothing to do with*
> *my Personal Self, my real ' I '... I value my body as my precious instrument*
> *of experience and of action in the outer world, but it is only an instrument*
> *... I treat it well, I seek to keep it in good health, but it is not my Self...*
> *I have a body, but I am more than my body...*

*I have emotions and feelings, but I am more than my emotions
and feelings... My emotions are diversified, changing, sometimes
contradictory... They may swing from love to hatred, from calm to anger,
from joy to sorrow, and yet my essence—my true nature—does not change
... ' I ' remain... Though a wave of anger may temporarily submerge me,
I know it will pass in time; therefore, I am not this anger ... Since I can
observe and understand my emotions, and then gradually learn to direct,
use and integrate them harmoniously, it is clear they are not my Self ... I
have emotions, but I am more than my emotions...*

*I have desires and impulses, but I am more than my desires and impulses...
Desires are aroused by physical and emotional drives, and by other
influences ... They are often changeable and contradictory therefore they
are not my Self ... I have desires, but I am more than my desires...*

*I have a mind and thoughts, but I am more than my mind and thoughts...
My mind is a valuable tool of discovery and expression, but it is not
the essence of my being... Its contents are constantly changing as it
embraces new ideas, knowledge and experience... Often it refuses to obey
me! Therefore, it cannot be me, my Self ... It is an organ of knowledge,
imagination and intuition in regard to both the outer and the inner worlds,
but it is not my Self ... I have a mind, but I am more than my mind...*

*I engage in various activities and play many roles in life... I must play these
roles and I willingly play them as well as possible, be it the role of son or
daughter, mother or father, wife or husband, teacher or student, artist
or executive ... But I am more than the son, the wife, and the artist...
These are roles, specific but partial roles, I am playing, agree to play and
can watch and observe myself playing... Therefore, I am not any of them ...
I am Self-identified, and I am not only the actor, but also the director of
the acting ...*

Section Two

*After disidentifying from my Personal Self, the 'I' from the contents of
consciousness, such as sensations, emotions, desires, impulses, thoughts
and roles, I recognize and affirm that I am a permanent centre of pure
Self-awareness, love and will, capable of observing, directing and using all
my psychological processes and my physical body...*
I have a body, but I am more than my body...
I have emotions, but I am more than my emotions...

I have desires, but I am more than my desires...
I have a mind, but I am more than my mind...
I have roles, but I am more than my roles...
I am 'I', a permanent centre of pure Self-awareness, love and will ...

Make whatever notes or drawings you wish of your experience with this exercise. Has it given you any new insights or awareness?

Most people take a long time to develop this kind of Self-awareness, and so it is perfectly all right and quite natural if you have not immediately experienced (to your satisfaction) the sense of your Personal Self. As with all the exercises in this book, you will gain greater benefit by regularly repeating it until it does become real to you.

Stepping Back

When we are able to step back completely from all our partial identifications, that which remains is our centre—not simply another image, subpersonality or role but our Personal Self: who we are in essence.

But how do we step back 'in real life' when confronted with problems and difficulties? How do we disidentify from ourself?

One way to step back is by observing ourself directly and objectively in the moment, and by asking ourself questions. What are we experiencing right now? What are we aware of? What are our feelings? Our thoughts? *Who*, what part of us—what subpersonality—is experiencing it? Why is it happening now? What is the lesson for us to learn? What message is our Divinity Within giving us through this experience? What is the hidden gift or benefit for us to find in it?

Turning within and focusing quietly on these questions and the answers which often come in the silence keeps us from becoming mired down in worry, confusion and indecision. To be sure, the issue is not automatically resolved. Our feelings and thoughts about it usually do not change instantly.

But remembering to ask these questions about an outer difficulty or an inner conflict gives us solid ground to stand on. It helps us examine our situation, identify options and choose to take action. It usually makes the situation more manageable. It helps us ultimately to benefit from the difficulty if possible, rather than to be drained or defeated by it. With a change in our own perspective, the difficulty can often turn into an opportunity.

Point of Power

When we become aware of our avoidance, resistance, fear or other blocks with any given issue (including bringing more love into our life), we can ask ourself what part of us, which subpersonality, is feeling it and why. Then if we wish, we may choose to *identify with it,* stepping into it and exaggerating it so as to experience it more fully and more deliberately, until we can begin to recognize and accept it.

Later we can choose to *disidentify from it,* stepping back from it to give us perspective to deal with it.

Therefore, we can choose to step into or out of our Personal Self or 'I' and *the act of choice becomes the point of power,* and not the avoidance, resistance, fear or other block itself. Making this choice leads to increased inner freedom and self-mastery.

There is great personal empowerment in Disidentification, as it shows us that *whatever we choose to step into, we can also choose to step out of* and thus we need no longer be afraid of our feelings, thoughts or any other parts of ourself. *The power and freedom to make this choice is always ours.*

A basic Psychosynthesis principle is that *we are dominated by everything with which we become identified, and can dominate, direct and utilize everything from which we disidentify.* Thus, our physical sensations, feelings, desires, thoughts, roles and other identifications need not control us, as they once might have done. We now have a way to regulate and use them more effectively.

Disidentification is the method which allows us to become free of the domination of all our partial images, including all our blocks to bringing more love into our life. It gives us the means to be free.

It allows us to *choose* to be free.

Thus, Disidentification has many values. It helps us to (a) step back from whatever we are feeling, thinking and identifying with; (b) observe, use and harmonize all parts of ourself; (c) experience who we are, a permanent centre of pure Self-awareness, love and will; and (d) rest, nurture and heal ourself.

However, the goal is not for us to be totally disidentified all the time. Rather it is to help us accept and express the gifts of *all* parts of ourself in ways which lead to self-mastery and wholeness.

EXERCISE: *Personal Self-Realization*

It can be reassuring to realize that our basic essential Self remains the same throughout our life, regardless of what is happening around us. To deepen your experience of your Personal Self, we present the following exercise adapted from a conception by Diana Whitmore in her book, *The Joy of Learning: A Guide to Psychosynthesis in Education.*

We suggest that you pre-record this exercise, on a digital device of your choice for ease of use. Avoid rushing through it. Take your time.

Close your eyes... Sit up straight... Take a few deep breaths ... Relax... Allow your body, emotions and thoughts to become still... Become like a calm, quiet lake...

When you are ready, allow to come into your awareness any memory from your early childhood... It may be a pleasant or an unpleasant one...

Take your time... Wait patiently in the silence, knowing something will soon come to you... Be willing to accept whatever comes without judging, censoring or rejecting it ... Simply be ready to observe and examine it ...

When you begin to sense something, allow specific details to come back to you... How old are you?... What clothes are you wearing?... Where are you?... What time of day is it?... What time of year?... Is anyone else around?... What is happening?... What do you see?... What can you hear?... How do you feel?... Observe the original experience with as many of your senses as you can... Allow it to be very real for you again, but avoid becoming lost in it ...

Ask yourself, who, what innermost place in me, had this experience originally?... Who was a child then?... Who is re-experiencing it now?... Who is aware now?... Who am I?...

Then allow to come to you any memory from your teenage years... Take your time... Wait patiently in the silence, knowing something will soon come to you... Be willing to accept whatever comes without judging, censoring or rejecting it ... Simply be ready to observe and examine it ... When you begin to sense something, allow specific details to come back to you... Observe the original experience with all your senses... Allow it to be very real for you again, but avoid becoming lost in it ...

Ask yourself, who, what innermost place in me, had this experience originally?... Who was an adolescent then?... Who is re-experiencing it now?... Who is aware now?... Who am I?...

Then allow to come to you any memory from the past week... Take your time... Wait patiently in the silence, knowing something will soon come to you... Be willing to accept whatever comes without judging, censoring or rejecting it ... Simply be ready to observe and examine it ...

When you begin to sense something, allow specific details to come back to you... Observe the original experience with as many of your senses as you can... Allow it to be very real for you again, but avoid becoming lost in it ...

Ask yourself, who, what innermost place in me, had this experience originally?... Who is re-experiencing it now?... Who is aware?... Who am I?...

Then allow to come to you any experience which may take place for you sometime in the future... Take your time... Wait patiently in the silence, knowing something will soon come to you... Be willing to accept whatever comes without judging, censoring or rejecting it... Simply be ready to observe and examine it...

When you begin to sense something, allow specific details to come to you... Observe the experience with as many of your senses as you can... Allow it to be very real for you, but avoid becoming lost in it ...

Ask yourself, who, what innermost place in me, is imagining this future experience now?... Who is aware now?... Who may experience it in the future?... Who has a future?... Who will be aware then?... Who am I?

Realize it has been one basic innermost place in you, the same 'you', who has had all these experiences... It is this singular 'you' who provides the continuity and the stability throughout your life... It is this 'you' who is at

the very centre of your being when all else is peeled away...
It is this 'you' who is pure, permanent and unchanging...
It is this 'you' who is your Personal Self ... It is this 'you' who is
connected directly to your Divinity Within ...

Make whatever notes or drawings you wish of your experience with this exercise. Has it given you any new insights or awareness?

Functions of the Personal Self

Our Personal Self has two primary functions. One, as we have seen in this chapter, is as an 'Observer' who objectively perceives and expresses *awareness*. But it is more than simply an impartial spectator. It also expresses the creative force of the *will,* which is the topic of Chapter Eight.

Ideally, it uses these two functions to bring together all our partial identifications into a unified, harmonious whole. Therefore, it is our Personal Self who is the conductor of the orchestra of our partial images, sub-personalities and roles. Harmonizing together, they perform the rhapsodic score composed for us by our Divinity Within.

Applying It

Here are a few suggestions for using Disidentification.

1. Verbal Affirmation

Repeat daily the full Personal Self-Awareness exercise presented earlier in this chapter. In addition, use this shortened form of the exercise several times throughout the day:

I have a body, but I am more than my body.
I have emotions, but I am more than my emotions.
I have desires, but I am more than my desires.
I have a mind, but I am more than my mind.
I have roles, but I am more than my roles.
I am I, a permanent centre of pure self-awareness, love and will.

2. The Observer

Immediately after making the affirmations above, take five minutes to observe yourself—such as your physical appearance, sensations and condition; your emotions and feelings, and how you experience and express them; your wants and desires, and how you satisfy them; your thoughts and ideas, and what they mean to you; your subpersonalities and roles, and how they influence you.

As you do so, say aloud over and over again, *'Now I am aware of...'* and finish the sentence with whatever you are aware of about yourself in that moment. Avoid making judgemental or critical statements. Develop your ability to be more discerning, accurate and objective about yourself, for when you do so, you begin to experience and express your Personal Self more deliberately and clearly.

3. Disidentification Reminder
Say to yourself regularly,

> *'I am more than whoever 'I' think 'I' am in any given moment, for I (as my Personal Self) know that 'I' am changing constantly from one subpersonality to another.'*

Suggested Reading
- *What We May Be,* by Piero Ferrucci, is an excellent practical manual for psychological and spiritual growth. It introduces clearly and simply the vision and major techniques of Psychosynthesis. It is the book we recommend highly to read first if you want to learn more about Psychosynthesis and how to apply its principles and methods in daily life.

Next in Chapter Eight we explore the way in which we make and implement decisions and how it affects the process of bringing more love into our life.

8

Choosing to Take Action

In this chapter we examine our process of making and implementing decisions so that we may strengthen our will to love more freely and fully.

Observations about Choice

This book states that bringing more love into our life is a deliberate action we can take. Like all personal actions, it requires us to make the choice to do it. Thus, knowing more about how we make choices and how we put them into action may aid in addressing our blocks to love.

- Some choices are simple to make, whereas others seem so difficult. The difficult ones are a test: Do we choose what is easy, comfortable and convenient, following the path of least resistance? Or do we use our will to summon the strength and courage we may need to move through our fears and deal directly with the situation?

- If we do not make a choice consciously, we end up making it unconsciously. In other words, our not deciding is deciding, after all.

- Where there is a *will,* there is a way. How willing are we to look for another way? How willing are we to make decisions and choices which enhance (rather than limit) our life?

- It sometimes takes honesty, openness and courage to make choices which support us—to say 'no' when it is easier for us to say 'yes'; to take a new and untried path; to live by our own values and priorities no matter what others may say.

- It empowers us to make free and deliberate choices, no matter how large or small they may be. Making choices allows us, as the Native Indians say, 'to stand firmly within our circle of power', expressing our freedom and independence, and exercising our capacity to get things done.

- A completely centred, deliberate and willed choice is one where, with detachment, we are able to choose to do something, or equally choose *not* to do it. It is a choice which is not conditioned by fears, impulsive desires or 'shoulds'. It is one which leads to greater freedom and independence, rather than to limitation or dependence. It is a responsible choice, neither harmful to ourself nor to others.

The Will

A Course in Miracles says we need to find all the barriers within ourself we have built against love. One aim of this book is to do precisely that. However, even when we know some of our barriers, we may have great difficulty in doing anything about them. What stops us from lessening or eliminating their influence upon us? What stops us from making and implementing the choice to bring more love into our life?

One answer may be that our blocks are stronger than our intention or will to overcome them. If so, then we need to develop our will as a step in choosing to love.

What is the will? It is *not* what has been termed 'Victorian will', that is, strong will-power, force, control, domination, manipulation or self-denial. It is *not* saying through clenched teeth, 'I *will* do this or that (if it kills me),' or, 'I *impose* my will upon you, whether you like it or not.' Neither is it an instinct, drive, urge or desire.

In *The Act of Will,* Roberto Assagioli, MD, says,

> "The true function of the will is not to act against the personality drives to *force* the accomplishment of one's purposes. The will has a *directive* and *regulatory* function; it balances and constructively utilizes all the other activities and energies of the human being without repressing any of them."

In its simplest form, then, *the act of will is the capacity to make a free and deliberate choice and then implement it effectively.* It is an act of volition designed to facilitate action.

The will is needed to mobilize all our personal resources and to initiate and integrate change. Therefore, the will is a good thing, and we need it to bring more love into our life.

Pure Forms and Distortions

The transpersonal quality of will can be experienced and expressed in many ways. Some ways may be considered pure, while others are distorted through our needs, desires and experience. The following list gives examples of both forms. To get a sense of the will and how you relate to it, consider for a moment how often you experience or express each of these qualities.

The Will

Pure Forms	Distortions
• Assertiveness/initiative	• Aggression/violence
• Concentration/focus	• Ambivalence/indecision
• Courage/daring	• Anger/resentment
• Decisiveness	• Domination/imposition
• Determination	• Fear of entrapment
• Discipline	• Fear of losing control
• Endurance/patience	• Helplessness/powerlessness
• Energy/dynamic power	• Manipulation
• Integration/synthesis	• Power-seeking
• Mastery	• Rebellion
• Order/organization	• Resistance
• Persistence/tenacity	• Rigidity
• Responsibility	• Stubbornness

The pure forms facilitate constructive action while the distortions either limit action or introduce destructive action.

The Process of Choosing

Some people *make* decisions and choices quite easily. They have their own method or process which works well for them.

Others have great difficulty. They are indecisive and cannot make up their mind. Or they are ambivalent and can appreciate all sides of an issue. Or they simply delay making a decision for as long as possible before committing themselves.

Some people *implement* or act upon their decisions and choices quite easily. They follow through from the original idea to its achievement with little difficulty. They breathe life into their decisions and then take the consequences.

Others always have difficulty in carrying out their decisions and choices. They habitually encounter blocks and limitations which keep their decisions from being implemented. They either do not act at all or fail to complete whatever they do begin or are unwilling to take responsibility for the consequences of their actions.

Some people make choices *rationally*. They define their needs, gather information, identify viable options, analyze and evaluate each of them and then finally make a logical deduction, usually whichever one seems 'best' or 'most appropriate' for them.

Others make choices *intuitively*. They sense whatever 'wants to happen' or 'feels right' to them in the moment, and they follow it without further consideration. These people may or may not then look for rational reasons to justify or support their intuitive choices.

Some people make choices rapidly, even spontaneously, while others delay making choices, keeping their options open for as long as they can.

Consider for a moment your response to the following questions about how you make and implement choices:

- What is your *primary* way of making decisions and choices?

- What prevents you from *making* decisions and choices more quickly and easily?

- What prevents you from *implementing* them more quickly and easily?

- What implications does your choice-making process have for the basic principle of this book, that is, you can *choose* to bring more love into your life?

- Have you actually made the choice yet to bring more love into your life?

We find that people typically respond to this last question from either their head (that is, with a thought) or their heart (an aspiration). However, the barriers and blocks to love usually reside within the solar plexus, the so-called pit of the stomach, where gut-level feelings, such as fears, are often experienced.

For many people—at least until they begin to strengthen their will—these gut-level feelings are so strong that they create powerful *resistances* which can weaken or render ineffective thoughts and other psychological functions. Put simply, fears can overpower thoughts and aspirations, just as one radio transmitter can jam another. Fortunately, however, we can use the will to stop this interference from happening.

Choice, Personal Resistance and Avoidance

Personal resistance is not the same as simple disagreement or difference of opinion. Rather it is an act of defiance, opposition or rebellion, often fuelled by fear. As we have already indicated, resistance is a distortion of the will. We usually experience it within ourself when we want to avoid something—a person, a situation, a problem or ourself. It can help us delay, deflect or sabotage something, even those things we say we want.

Our resistance patterns usually start in childhood in response to a need to protect ourself, and we then carry them with us into adulthood, long after we have outgrown the original need. They often become a habitual way of behaving.

In the short term our resistance helps us to feel safer and in control, and therefore more comfortable, or at least, less uncomfortable. In the long term, however, it robs us of freedom of choice as well as a sense of fulfilment. A 'loyal soldier' defending us against 'the enemy' for most of our life, our resistance can be retired from 'active duty' as we become aware that the 'war' is over.

Resistance takes many different forms. The following list presents a small sample. Which ones do you experience as part of your avoidance patterns?

Boredom and Impatience. We resist either by deadening ourself through apathy and monotony, or by becoming eternally restless.

Confusion and Indecision. We never have to *do* anything as long as we remain in a constant state of upheaval, crisis or bewilderment.

Indulgence. We resist by allowing ourself to be dominated and controlled by our selfishness, laziness or other self-serving desires.

Intellectualization. We read books, attend lectures, take courses, keep journals, discuss, analyze and evaluate—but keeping it all safely on the intellectual level to avoid having to *do* anything about making changes in our life.

Invisibility. We withdraw quietly to the background, contribute little and may engage in silent sabotage or passive aggression.

Judgement. We find ways to make others or things 'wrong' or 'bad', and thus give ourself good reason to keep them at a safe, manageable distance.

Lack of Commitment. By withholding commitment, we seek to avoid the possibility of risk, responsibility and both failure and success.

Procrastination. We create circumstances to delay our having to confront a person, a situation or a problem.

Rationalization. We find good 'reasons' for doing whatever we want to do and avoiding everything else.

Rebellion. We are quick to express our righteous indignation and act in defiance of whatever we wish to avoid. 'Nobody is going to tell *me* what to do!'

Victimization. As long as we can feel we are a victim of circumstances and have someone or something else to blame for our situation, we can avoid being accountable for who we are and how we live our life.

Work and Activity. We obligate ourself with responsibilities and so stay busy, occupied, distracted and unavailable.

How else do you avoid things?

EXERCISE: *The Act of Will*

Now we explore the act of will itself and invite you to test the method by applying it to the issue of choosing to love. In Psychosynthesis the act of will is divided into six successive stages:

- Exploring a purpose to be achieved
- Deliberating upon it
- Choosing to do it
- Affirming our intention to do it
- Planning how to do it
- Executing or implementing it

Obviously, we do not move deliberately through all these stages for everyday choices we make, nor is there a need to do so. *However, we do suggest that you use all these stages when considering an important issue or change in your life.*

The value of this method is that it empowers us, strengthens our will and helps us to achieve our purpose systematically.

People are usually more effective with some of these stages than with others. By exploring and experiencing one stage at a time, you may discover weaknesses in your decision-making and decision-implementing process and can then take steps to strengthen them.

STAGE ONE

Exploring a Purpose to Be Achieved

The first stage in the act of will is to identify a specific purpose you wish to achieve. For this exercise we suggest that you find a purpose which would help you to counteract your *blocks* to love, for example, 'to increase my self-esteem, to demonstrate more faith and trust, to communicate more honestly and openly, to reach out and make new friends or to take more risks'.

As you explore, make certain you find a purpose you feel enthusiastic about, one you feel is quite worthwhile and important, something you definitely intend to achieve. State it clearly and precisely, beginning with, *'I use my will to...'*

Next, what are your motives or reasons for wishing to achieve this particular purpose? What will it give you—what are its benefits, values and advantages to you? Knowing its potential rewards serves to motivate you and keep your interest high.

STAGE TWO

Deliberating upon Your Purpose

The second stage in the act of will is to consider the various ways you may achieve your purpose—actions, activities and projects—together with their likely outcomes and consequences, so that you may choose deliberately the best available option from a wide range of possibilities.

One method of deliberation is to brainstorm ways to achieve your purpose. Remember from Chapter One, that in brainstorming the point is to allow many ideas to come to you as quickly as possible.

Now is *not* the time to evaluate, judge or reject any idea. (You may do so later.) Rather, include everything as it occurs spontaneously to you. Enjoy your creativity and originality. Allow yourself to be inspired. Avoid rushing through the exercise. Take your time.

Then examine your responses. Mark all the ideas you feel are worth considering to implement. Explore their likely consequences, both favourable and unfavourable, and consider how willing you are to accept full responsibility for them.

Next, as a part of your deliberation, turn within to your inner source of wisdom to seek information, guidance and support concerning the purpose you have chosen and the various options you have identified for achieving it.

To facilitate this process, use the Attunement Exercise from Chapter Three. In addition, you may also wish to use the Receptive and Reflective Meditations found in Chapter Four.

If you are a member of a supportive group, such as a meditation, prayer or study group, you may also wish to take your deliberation into the group for review.

From our experience of living in community at the Findhorn Foundation, we know involving a *sympathetic* group of others can be very helpful in all stages of the act of will.

STAGE THREE

Choosing to Do It

Sooner or later the deliberation stage must be brought to an end, and therefore the third stage in the act of will is to make a choice among the options. It means deciding upon one of them and discarding the others.

Now choose the one option you prefer for achieving your purpose, one which has realistic possibilities of success, and one (for the purpose of this exercise), you can achieve within the next few days.

Write it down clearly and precisely, beginning with, '*I use my will to...*' together with any feelings or thoughts you have about the option and your process of choosing it.

STAGE FOUR

Affirming Your Intention

The fourth stage in the act of will is to affirm your intention and commitment to achieving your purpose. You may feel this stage is unnecessary, and yet by now you are aware how resistance can sabotage or defeat your best efforts.

Create an affirmation which reflects your willingness to achieve your purpose. Write it down, beginning with, '*I, (Name),...*' Use your affirmation regularly until you achieve your purpose. Remember that visualizing the successful outcome of your purpose as you write and say your affirmation also helps you to manifest it.

STAGE FIVE

Planning How to Achieve Your Purpose

The fifth stage in the act of will is to prepare a detailed plan for achieving your purpose. Like Stage Two, this stage involves deliberation, but in very specific terms, and directed towards only one option.

Now formulate a plan for achieving your purpose. Include such factors as: what specific steps you will take and in what sequence; when you will take them, their timing and their duration; where you will take them; who else is involved or needs to be considered; which resources you require: equipment, materials, money, space, time; how you will evaluate your efforts: criteria to use to measure your success.

Consider for a moment how you could sabotage or defeat your efforts towards achieving your purpose. How might your resistance show itself? If it does, how will you deal with it? Will you allow it to stop you? Or will you make a deliberate choice (an act of will) to acknowledge the resistance, and then proceed despite it?

Visualize regularly in graphic detail the successful achievement of your purpose. Vividly imagine its ideal resolution. As you do so, allow feelings of enthusiasm, determination and expectancy to grow within you.

Remember always to feel and think positively about your purpose and its successful outcome.

STAGE SIX

Implementing Your Plan

The final stage in the act of will is to direct the execution of your plan, skillfully calling upon all your inner resources in support of your purpose: sensory perceptions, emotions and feelings, desires and drives, intellect, imagination and intuition.

Avoid manipulating, imposing or forcing anything to happen. Rather, maintain a clear, positive intention, remain flexible and facilitate the achievement of your purpose.

Assessing the Outcome

How successful were you in achieving your purpose, as measured by your criteria? What did you learn from the action you took? Which of the stages in the act of will were you most comfortable with, and which ones triggered resistance or other problems?

Which stages may account for your difficulties in addressing your blocks to love? Note any other observations you wish to make about your experience of making a considered, free and deliberate act of will.

An Act of Will Empowers and Frees

In summary, this six-stage process is an empowering one, as it strengthens and trains our capacity to make free and deliberate choices and to put them into action effectively. As the ladder of Chapter One suggests, using the will to make choices which empower and serve us brings us greater freedom. It also helps us to experience our Personal Self.

Recall from Chapter Seven, that the two functions of the Personal Self are to express awareness and will.

Applying It

Roberto Assagioli, MD, observes, "Every act of the will trains the will, and each bit of training allows for further acts of will." Piero Ferrucci calls this synergistic interaction a "virtuous circle".

Here are a few suggestions for training the will.

1. Daily Record

Keep a record of a few of the choices you make. Record relevant details, such as how you make the choice, who (what part of you—which sub-personality) makes the choice and who implements it, the nature of any resistance you may experience to making or implementing it, how the choice (and the process you use to make it) empowers and serves you or disempowers and limits you.

2. Deliberate Choices

Make and implement a series of deliberate choices, and voice them aloud. For example, 'Now I choose to close this book. Now I choose to stand up. Now I choose to make myself a cup of tea. Now I choose to walk into the kitchen. Now I choose to open the cupboard. Now I choose to take out a cup.'

Make your every act the result of a totally willed, deliberate, explicit choice. One value of this exercise is that it helps to experience how habitual and automatic our actions usually are.

3. Action ('Acting As If') Affirmation

Then follow the above exercise by behaving 'as if' you already fully possessed the desired personal empowerment and its qualities of authority, confidence and independence. How do you sit, stand, walk, speak? What other external, physical gestures, postures and actions can you take?

Create and express all the outer signs of personal empowerment. Then notice if maintaining the outward physical signs results in corresponding inner feelings. Refer to the original instructions for this technique in Chapter Five.

4. Dialogue with Your Personality and Will

Write or improvise an imaginary dialogue between your personality (or any of your subpersonalities) and your will. How do they relate to each other? What do they have to say to each other? Choose the format you would like the dialogue to follow: perhaps a telephone conversation, a magazine interview or a one-act stage, radio or television play.

5. Personal Goal

Consider various simple, specific, observable actions you could take 'in real life' within the next seven days which would be a step towards bringing more love into your life. Then choose one which seems important to you, one to take as a personal goal. Make a deliberate choice to achieve it. Write it down as a reminder to yourself.

Remember, making choices strengthens the will, which in turn makes it easier to make choices. Keep practising making choices, as often, freely and deliberately as you can.

Suggested Reading

- *The Act of Will,* by Roberto Assagioli, MD, the inspiration for this chapter, examines aspects of the will (strong will, skillful will, good will, Transpersonal Will, Universal Will); the many qualities, or pure forms of the will; and the stages of willing. It concludes, "Since the outcome of successful willing is the satisfaction of one's needs, we can see the act of will is essentially joyous. And the realization of the Self, or more exactly of being a Self, gives a sense of freedom, of power, of mastery which is profoundly joyous."

  Relevant to the theme of this book, Dr. Assagioli says, "To cultivate human love that is satisfying, enduring and creative is truly an art. Human love is not simply a matter of feeling, an affective condition or disposition. To love *well* calls for all that is demanded by the practice of any art, indeed of any human activity, namely an adequate measure of discipline, patience and persistence. All these we have seen to be qualities of the will."

  Thus, deliberately choosing to love is an act of will.

Next in Chapter Nine we explore the topics of change and maintenance and their influence upon our choosing to love.

9

Choosing to Change

In this chapter we examine how the way we relate to change and maintenance affects the way we relate to love. The effective use of change and its polar opposite, maintenance, is needed if we are to open ourself to giving and receiving love more freely and fully.

What Is Change?

Change is simply a difference of some kind, a movement or shift from one thing to another. Change can be gradual or instantaneous, subtle or intense, minor or major in its impact. Change brings challenge, disorder, instability and the unknown. Change also allows for newness, growth, progress and evolution. Most people are more aware of change than they are of maintenance, and yet, in its way, maintenance also affects our bringing more love into our life.

What Is Maintenance?

Maintenance is the opposite of change. We talk of home maintenance and maintenance of the status quo or keeping everything the same as it is now. Thus, maintenance is simply a conservation, a continuation or a preservation. It respects, embraces and carries on with the present moment as it is, without making any changes.

Change and maintenance are at opposite ends of the same spectrum, and we generally feel more at ease with one than with the other.

For example, some people are quite comfortable with change and may even find it attractive. They are usually impatient or restless with the status quo and seek the freedom and stimulation which change offers them. They find it easy and enlivening to take risks. They often pursue change for the sake of change and feel a need to keep moving on to what is new.

Others at the opposite end of the spectrum are quite comfortable with maintenance and may even find it very attractive. They are usually doubtful or fearful of change, and seek the order, stability and security which the status quo offers them. They find it difficult and challenging to take risks. They often resist change simply because it is a change and feel a need to continue and preserve whatever is known and familiar to them. As with most personal characteristics, we usually express a mixture of both of these polarities. We may pursue change in one part of our life, such as in our work, while we pursue maintenance in another part, such as in personal relationships.

Pure Forms and Distortions

The transpersonal qualities of change and maintenance can be experienced and expressed in many ways. Some ways may be considered pure, while others are distorted through our experience, needs and desires. The list below gives examples of both forms. To get a sense of them and how you relate to them, consider how often you experience or express each quality.

How we relate to change and maintenance affects the way we relate to our specific barriers and blocks to love and our willingness (or unwillingness) to overcome them.

Resistance Causes Pain

There are times when it is easy to change, and we simply flow with the changes. But there also are painful times when we resist making necessary changes, and we go along reluctantly, kicking and screaming all the way.

However, it is usually not the nature of the change, but our resistance to it which causes the pain. A change is a problem only if *we* make it one. So, as we learn to flow with the changes without fear or resistance, life becomes much easier. We can learn how to read the warning signs and 'collaborate with the inevitable' in order to avoid our resistance and the pain and suffering it causes. We can remember philosopher Ivan Illich's observation, "Pain is human; suffering is a performance."

Change

Pure Forms	Distortions
• Creativity	• Dissipation of energy
• Enthusiasm	• Fear of entrapment
• Freedom	• Fear of limitation
• Growth	• Impatience/restlessness
• Spontaneity	• Inconsistency
• Vitality	• Scatteredness/ungroundedness

Maintenance	
Pure Forms	**Distortions**
• Containment	• Attachments
• Duty/loyalty	• Boredom
• Grounding	• Closed-mindedness
• Honouring of tradition	• Fear of letting go
• Order	• Fear of the unknown
• Peace	• Inertia/lazines
• Stability/strength	• Rigidity/resistance

Change Offers Gifts

It is amazing how soon we can get used to change as long as we have the courage and conviction that the change which is taking place is all for the very best. It means accepting that a perfect pattern runs through our life, and each change which comes is a part of our Divinity Within plan for us. We can get used to change much more easily when we remember to accept change as a *gift* from our Divinity Within, offering lessons, insights and growth.

So, one challenge of change is not to look for ways to deal with the difficulties we may associate with change, but rather to be open to accept the *gifts* which change brings. The question is, can we accept each change in our life as a stepping stone to something new and more wonderful—and not as a stumbling block to trip us up? Can we accept each change as a blessing?

Another challenge is to honour and keep in our life whatever is necessary and desirable *while* making changes. Making a change only for the sake of change can be a sign of restlessness or impatience, and can bring instability, confusion and even chaos. The challenge is to be open to change, even to invoke change, while also knowing what to *maintain* in our life, and to do it within the midst of change.

When we experience a change as a crisis, a helpful image from Psychosynthesis suggests that a personal crisis is simply our Divinity Within knocking on the door of our personality, trying to get our attention, and saying, 'Come on, it's time for you to take another step. It's time for you to grow. It's time for you to be more of who you are. I am here. I will help you.'

EXERCISE: *The Challenge of Change*

This exercise is designed to help you feel more comfortable with change and the gifts it brings. It provides you with helpful insights about any change in your life and guides you step by step through it.

You may use this exercise to address a change already in your life, a change on its way to you or a change you would like to come into your life. We suggest that you pre-record this exercise on a device of your choosing, and that you have writing materials nearby to make notes of your responses to certain questions. Avoid rushing through it. Take your time.

Close your eyes... Sit up straight... Take a few deep breaths... Relax... Allow your body, emotions and thoughts to become still... Become like a calm, quiet lake...

Release as much as possible whatever feelings and thoughts you may have about change... Let them go... For now, give yourself permission simply to accept change as something normal, natural and necessary...

Allow to come to you a memory of a major change you once went through, and how you experienced it at the time... Recall the good which has come to you from it...

Now choose a change within yourself which you need to make before you can bring more love into your life...

Focus your attention upon the exact nature of the change... What precisely is happening, or what do you want to happen?...

What is this change asking of you?...

Allow to come to you two or three benefits this change could bring into your life...

What are your feelings and thoughts about this change?...

Are you aware of any fear, resistance or other negative feeling within you concerning this change?... If so, what is its source—where does it come from?...

Recognize that this negativity limits you and your relationships... Choose to take action despite its influence upon you... Affirm your willingness to move beyond it...

Then affirm your openness and willingness to make this change...

What is the ideal resolution of this change—how would you like it to turn out?...

Take a few moments now to visualize this ideal resolution unfolding successfully step by step, and so help to bring it about... Picture it in great detail... Experience it vividly...

What is a practical 'next step' you can take concerning this change?...

Are you willing to commit yourself to take this step?... If you are visualize yourself taking this specific step successfully...

Then imagine having moved through the entire change... What has the change done for you—what is its gift to you?... How are you and your life different, especially your relationships?...

If this change were a stepping stone to something greater in your life, what might that be?...

Next attune to your inner source of wisdom to seek information, guidance and support concerning this change...

(Remain in the silence for as long as you wish.)

In your own time, allow everything to fade... Bring your attention back to the room where you are now... Open your eyes... Take a deep breath... And a gentle stretch...

Make whatever notes or drawings you wish of your experience with this exercise. Has it given you any new insights or awareness?

Forgiveness

One change we usually need to make before we can bring more love into our life involves forgiveness. We hold on to past hurt, close down and shut off emotionally to protect ourself and become unavailable psychologically both to give and to receive love.

Many people find forgiveness very powerful. Why? It is because they discover that the act of forgiveness helps them to change.

What is forgiveness? The book *A Course in Miracles* says, 'Forgiveness is letting go the past. Forgiveness is letting go of whatever we think people, the world or God has done to us, as well as whatever we think we have done to them.' Forgiveness then is an act of release. Therefore, a change of heart and mind is the first step in forgiveness, whether we are directing it towards ourself or others.

Forgiveness Heals

The greatest act of healing is the act of forgiveness. It is also one of the most difficult. Forgiveness helps us to empty out the old to make room for the new. It empties out the old anger, blame, fear, guilt and pain, and makes room for the new freedom, vitality, joy, love and peace.

Forgiveness is an act of self-kindness, a gift to ourself. It may also heal the other person, but *ultimately forgiveness is done for ourself, to heal ourself, to free ourself.* Forgiveness does not imply, 'I will forgive you if you do this or that...' but 'I will forgive you because I must, if I ever hope to continue to live freely and fully again.'

A word of caution is necessary. If we believe that we have forgiven someone, but are indifferent towards that person, it is not true forgiveness. If we believe we have forgiven someone and now we avoid seeing that person, it is not true forgiveness.

True forgiveness is releasing our hurt, releasing the past, and feeling towards that person now as we felt before the situation occurred. True forgiveness allows others to be themselves. As Mother Teresa of Calcutta said, "To forgive takes love; to forget takes humility."

All forgiveness starts with self-forgiveness. Only then can we forgive others.

We need to accept the past. Then we need to let it all go so we can accept who and where we are today, *now*. Why cling to pain? Why cling to the past? Why hold on to the very thing which keeps us from love!

We need to have mercy on ourself and others. We need to allow ourself to come back into our own heart. Allow ourself to be healed. Allow ourself to be free. Allow ourself to love and be loved.

Forgiveness is the key which unlocks the door to bringing more love into our life. It is a powerful method we can *choose* to use whenever we are willing to let go of the past, and move freely and expectantly into a more whole, more fulfilling future.

Applying It

Here are a few suggestions for dealing with change, maintenance and forgiveness.

1. Act of Will

(a) Make a deliberate act of will to *change* something in your life, for example, a habit, pattern or routine, such as how you bathe and dress yourself, how and what you eat, the route you take when you go out or whatever you do in your spare time. Then notice how you feel about making the change.

(b) Also make a deliberate act of will to *maintain* something in your life, for example, to do something for a longer period of time than you would prefer, to delay something you would prefer to do now, to honour a tradition or to perform an act of duty or loyalty. Then notice how you feel about the act of maintenance.

2. Daily Risks

At least once an hour (set your watch, phone or kitchen timer), ask yourself, *'What risk do I need to be taking right now?'*

Then take at least one risk each day.

3. Forgiveness Prayer

Remember to use prayer. We can pray to the Divinity Within, asking for help. Here is a short, simple prayer we find helpful.

'Today I ask the Divinity Within me
to help me to forgive completely.
Here is my heart. Cleanse it.
Renew my spirit so I may be loving to everyone.
I no longer want to hold anyone in judgement and condemnation.
I let your love move in and through me,
So I may willingly forgive and forget all offences completely.
I am grateful for your help.
Thank you.'

4. Altar Exercise

Use this visualization exercise *only after you have done all you can do* to resolve and heal a challenge with another person or a particular situation in your life.

Visualize a large altar standing before you. Experience yourself taking the person or situation troubling you to the altar and lay the person or situation upon the altar.

Then, as you move away from the altar, say to the Divinity Within, *'I cannot do anything more with this situation. I hand it over to you and release it. Please take it.'*

Say it with your whole heart. As you do so, open yourself to something happening between you and the Divinity Within you. Open to the feeling that a heavy burden is being lifted from you, and you are free of it. Then give thanks.

Suggested Reading

- *A Course in Miracles* says there are only two emotions: love and fear. Aggression, resentment, separation and guilt are all guises adopted by fear. Joy, forgiveness and peace of mind are all aspects of love. The miracles it teaches are the shifts in perception which enable us to view the world through the eyes of love, rather than through the eyes of fear. The book focuses upon forgiveness as a central theme, and it includes 365 daily lessons providing practical application of its teachings.

- *Cutting the Ties That Bind,* by Phyllis Krystal, says, "In order to be completely free, we need to be detached from anyone or anything which binds or dominates us, or in which we seek to find security in preference to the High C [Higher Consciousness] within each of us."

Next in Chapter Ten we explore the differences between conditional and unconditional love.

10

Choosing to Love
Unconditionally

In this chapter we explore bringing more unconditional love into our life.

The World Needs Unconditional Love

"Can you say to me and I say to you, 'I love you,' without either
of us feeling uncomfortable, threatened or that something is
expected of either of us? Can we love each other, regardless of
our age, sex or origin, with pure, understanding love?
With unconditional love? The world needs this sort of love.
All humanity needs this sort of love. Can we love this way?
We can, but it is not something simply to be talked about.
It is something to be acted upon, to be experimented with."

— EILEEN CADDY

Unconditional love is loving people freely, fully and openly, with no expectations, demands or restrictions. It gives total acceptance and respect and does not criticize or judge. Unconditional love is constant and is not turned on and off as in conditional love. Conditional love refers to placing restrictions on who or when we are willing to love. It is loving people only when they meet certain conditions we impose upon them and withholding or withdrawing our love when our conditions are not met.

Conditions, Expectations and Demands

As we love—a partner, family member, friend or another—most of us have unmet needs which result in our making certain demands of others. The less we are able to get our needs met in healthy, appropriate ways, the more demanding we are. We may express our demands quite clearly and directly, or we may hold on to them silently within ourself. We consider our demands valid, reasonable and necessary requirements before we open ourself to love.

How about you? Do you have any of the following expectations, conditions or demands about loving yourself and others?

I Will Love You Only If You...
- Accept and respect me just as I am.
- Acknowledge, encourage and understand me.
- Adore me, consider me attractive, capable, intelligent, responsible, wonderful.
- Agree with me and allow me to have my own way.
- Amuse me, entertain me and keep me from being bored.
- Are faithful to me, good to me, loyal to me and true to me.
- Are absolutely perfect and live up to all my expectations.
- Communicate honestly and openly with me.
- Do things for me (errands/favours/chores).
- Give me what I want from you (babies/money/sex/trinkets).
- Have things in common with me, share my beliefs, interests and values.
- Listen to me, follow my advice and do what I tell you to do.
- Love me in return.
- Make me feel good, happy, needed, secure and special.
- Prove to me you deserve my love and trust.
- Provide me with companionship and keep me from being lonely.
- Put me first in your life.
- Satisfy me and fulfil all my needs.
- Take care of me and protect me.
- Treat me as an adult and as an equal.
- Do not annoy or irritate me.
- Do not ask me to make commitments.
- Do not expect me to take unwanted responsibility.
- Do not cause me problems or trouble.
- Do not condemn, criticize, demean or judge me.
- Do not hurt me or cause me pain.
- Do not lie to me.
- Do not question or challenge me.
- Do not reject me or walk out on me.
- Do not take me for granted.

- Do not try to change me or ask me to change.
- Do not manipulate, use or abuse me.
- Do not make any such demands on *me!*

How do you give your love—with conditions or without them? Be honest but avoid judging either yourself or the ideal of unconditional love.

Conditional and Unconditional Love

Some people give their love to others only when such conditions are met. They withdraw their love when these conditions are unmet or violated. They choose very carefully whom they love. Their love is conditional.

Others give their love freely, fully and openly without such conditions, expectations or demands tied to it. They do not withdraw their love because of who others may be or what they may do. They do not choose whom to love, but keep their love flowing out to everyone equally. Their love is unconditional.

To take stock of how we relate to unconditional love in all our relationships, we can ask ourself the following questions:

- Can I be myself at all times?
- Can I allow others to be themselves without criticizing, judging or condemning them?
- Can I love and love and go on loving someone, asking nothing in return?
- Can I love someone with the same depth, and to the same degree, regardless of whether we are together or apart?
- Can I still love someone when I do not like or approve of something that person has said or done?
- Can I love someone enough that I can cease helping that person because I know if I go on helping, I will hold up that person's growth and evolution?
- Can I love someone enough that I can let that person go to grow and mature?
- Can I love someone enough that I can accept that person leaving me for someone else and hold no bitterness, resentment or jealousy?
- Can I love everyone equally, acknowledging our unity and interconnectedness?

Divine Love

Unconditional love is an expression of the Divinity within each one of us. Unconditional love is an all-embracing love. It gives acceptance, if not always approval, to everyone and everything. It is unique and universal, within reach of all of us. It is vitalizing. It is nurturing. It expects or demands absolutely nothing in return. It is its own reason for being.

We all have a tremendous job to do. It is the silent task of creating more and more unconditional love in the world. It is like the yeast in a lump of bread dough which does its job very quietly and silently without any fuss. Yet without it the bread would be a solid lump. As we begin to love unconditionally, so will the heaviness in our own life be lightened.

But if we love solely from the emotional level, then we are expecting something in return. Our love is then conditional, and is often possessive, indulgent, needy or sentimental. As long as we function principally from the emotional level, we are slaves to our emotions, puppets on the strings of our emotions, in one melodrama or soap opera after another.

Experience of Freedom

When we function from the level of unconditional love, recognizing and giving thanks to the Divinity Within as the source of this divine love, we begin to experience the meaning of freedom, and we are no longer tied up in knots emotionally.

How few of us function from this level! When we do, how often we are misunderstood by those people who function principally from the emotional level! How complicated relationships become when they can be simple and straightforward – all the more reason for us to change our outlook, our whole way of thinking, if necessary, and so help those around us to change their way of thinking.

Unconditional love does not come all at once. It starts in small ways and then grows one step at a time. Its benefits are enormous. Life is more abundant and fulfilling when we choose unconditional love as the primary principle which guides us. It is a deliberate *choice* we can make, one which serves us, everyone around us and the very planet Earth itself. We transform the world as we transform ourself with the power of unconditional love.

Where to Begin?

Some people say unconditional love is far too idealistic for them to achieve, and they would only be inviting failure if they ever were to try. They feel it is a concept which is so far above and beyond them they would not know even where or how to begin to develop it within themselves.

The place to begin is *here*. The time to begin is *now*. The way to begin is to *choose* to give unconditional love a high priority in our life.

More and more we are shown that life on our planet is one vast interconnected whole. The farthest person from us on Earth is only a telephone call away, a computer link away, a text, a twitter, a satellite radio or television transmission away. The billions of us who inhabit planet Earth are now inextricably interconnected by technology. But we have always been interconnected by other 'inner technology' as well: the farthest person is also only a kind and loving thought away, a quiet meditation away, a simple prayer away, a creative visualization away.

EXERCISE: *Loving Unconditionally*

Therefore, we present an exercise to give you an inner experience of unconditional love. We suggest that you pre-record this exercise. Give yourself at least 20 minutes to complete it. Avoid rushing through it. Take your time.

> *Find a comfortable position, sitting up straight... Close your eyes... Take several slow, deep breaths... Continue to breathe slowly and deeply...*
>
> *Observe your body... Do whatever is necessary to be completely free and relaxed physically...*
>
> *Observe your emotions... Whatever feelings you may be experiencing, pleasant or unpleasant, simply release them for the moment... They are your reactions to whatever is happening in your life, and you will not need them for this visualization... Do whatever is necessary to be completely free and relaxed emotionally...*
>
> *Observe your mind... Do the same with any thoughts you may be thinking... Release them as well... You do not need your intellect and*

its analytical and critical nature to distract you... Do whatever is necessary to be completely free and relaxed intellectually... Release, relax and let go...

When you are ready, focus your attention inside your body to where your heart is... For a moment put your hand over your heart and feel it beating... Within your heart is the seed of divine love, of unconditional love... Experience it now for yourself by imagining what it is like... Perhaps for you it is a colour... A feeling... A radiance... A vibration... A warmth... A wave...

At first experience it on its own, unrelated to anyone or anything... Allow pure love to be with you now...

Whatever you are experiencing now, no matter how subtle or indistinct it may be, imagine it as love... Sense it as love... Trust it as love... Accept it as love... Take it as your own inner experience of love... Use it for now as your personal reference of what unconditional love is for you...

Accept it for what it truly is: divine love, all-embracing love, universal vitalizing, nurturing love... Love which expects nothing in return... Love which gives compassionate acceptance and respect to everyone and everything...

Allow this unconditional love within you to radiate slowly throughout your whole being... Feel it filling you... Feel it enfolding you... Feel loving yourself unconditionally... Accepting yourself... Trusting yourself... Forgiving yourself... Appreciating yourself... Feel this unconditional love healing... Balancing... And making whole every part of your being...

Sense this unconditional love gradually expanding outward beyond yourself, until it fills the entire room where you are now... As you do, expand your awareness with it... Move with it... Grow with it... Feel being part of it... Experience this unconditional love overflowing into the entire building, and then beyond it...

Love is given to us so we may share it with others, so begin to sense this unconditional love radiating into your community... Sense it filling and enfolding all those you love... Your family... Your friends... Sense it filling and enfolding anyone you may dislike or are having problems with at this time... Allow unconditional love to come back to you from each person as well... Feel the healing power of unconditional love bringing you together in unity with everyone and everything...

Sense all these separate streams coming together into a single flow of love... As you do, experience unconditional love being both unique and universal... Sense this unconditional love expanding and radiating to the whole country... As you do, feel connected with it...

Sense this unconditional love expanding and radiating to the whole planet... As you do, feel and accept your oneness with it...

Sense this unconditional love expanding and radiating to the whole universe... As you do, feel and accept your wholeness...

Sense this unconditional love expanding and radiating to the whole cosmic creation... As you do, feel and accept your perfection...

Sense this unconditional love expanding and radiating to embrace the whole heart and mind of God... As you do, feel and accept your own divine essence...

Slowly bring your attention back to your own presence... As you do, experience the unconditional love you have been feeling as being entirely within your heart, where, in fact, it has always been centred, and will always be... Know that wherever you may be or whatever is happening to you, this love remains within your heart, ready to bring you the peace you are feeling right now...

Be aware also that you may draw upon its limitless supply any time you want, simply by choosing to do so... Trust that you may repeat as often as you like this experience of linking up on the inner planes of Spirit with everyone and everything with unconditional love...

In your own time, open your eyes, and as you do, bring the unconditional love you are feeling now with you... Bring it out... Externalize it...

Continue to experience it fully... Accept it as an expression of who you are at the very centre of your being, and who everyone else is as well... As you feel this unconditional love within you now, know also that you are feeling the God within you, for God is love...

Make whatever notes or drawings you wish of your experience with this exercise. Has it given you any new insights or awareness?

Service to Others

Why strive for unconditional love? It is because we do not love unconditionally for love's sake. Rather we love unconditionally as an act of *service*, a way of giving freely of ourself, a way of serving one another, humanity and the world.

For a time comes in our personal development when we realize that we are not isolated, independent individuals, but rather that we are all interdependent. We then experience genuine care and concern for others, become more aware of the larger whole and feel a deep desire to share our riches, whatever they may be, with others.

Humanitarian Albert Schweitzer observed, "I don't know what your destiny will be, but one thing I know: the only ones among you who will be really happy are those who have sought and found how to serve." True service is being who we are at all times and expressing as best we can our inherent transpersonal qualities, including unconditional love. The process of evolution engages us all to be conscious co-operators with it, and so we begin to see the needs of the whole and direct our resources to meet those needs.

The key to service is doing what we *want* to do, not *have* to do, in an effortless way. A Psychosynthesis trainer we know suggests two guiding principles when deciding what to do in life:

- Make a contribution.
- Do it whole-heartedly one hundred per cent.

We may ask ourself, '*How* can I best serve, *where* can I contribute, *what* is the greatest need, *where* can I give one hundred per cent?' A popular saying provides the answer, 'Ask not what the world needs; ask rather what makes your heart sing and go do that. For what the world needs is people with hearts that sing.'

Applying It

Here are a few suggestions for bringing more unconditional love into your life.

1. Affirmation

To avoid judging, criticizing and condemning others, affirm silently to yourself whenever you are tempted to think unkindly towards someone, *'I love you, I bless you, I see the divinity within you.'* Remind yourself to look beyond all outer appearances. Recognize and appreciate people for who they are—a permanent centre of pure Self-awareness, love and will.

2. Creative (Ideal Model) Visualization

Imagine how you would ideally like to express unconditional love—not a model of perfection, but a realistic and attainable ideal. Then visualize and experience yourself being this ideal. Move slowly scene by scene through a full day's activities, including interactions with others at work, leisure and home. Refer to the complete instructions for this exercise in Chapter Four.

3. Angels and Mortals

Each year in early December, Findhorn Foundation members take part in a festive ritual called 'Angels and Mortals'. They write their names on slips of paper and put them into a hat. When everyone has done so, each then draws out a name and becomes an instant 'angel' for their 'mortal' so chosen. Thus, everyone is both a mortal, and an angel for another mortal.

From then until Christmas, the angels' task is to love, appreciate and bless their mortals in as many different ways as they can imagine—anonymously; mortals never know who their angels are until Christmas morning. Angels find creative ways, as well as willing helpers, to let their mortals know they are being watched over by caring guardian angels.

Whatever form they take, these are all acts of unconditional love because all participants must trust, as mortals, that they will receive the full and loving attention of their angel, *independent* of however much they may do for their own adopted mortal. Thus, their attention can be focused more upon giving rather than receiving. In this ritual, as well as in life, when everyone gives, everyone receives.

To practise unconditional love, we invite you to become an 'angel' for someone! Do not wait until Christmas. Do it now. Choose a 'mortal', perhaps someone in your family, church or meditation group, a co-worker, a neighbour or whoever delivers your post, and begin to find ways to acknowledge, appreciate and do simple little things for the person—all anonymously, of course.

If you feel shy, awkward or embarrassed about following this suggestion, remember you are doing it for the other person, not for yourself. It need not take a great expenditure of time, money or effort—only love: Do not hold yourself back. Open your heart and focus upon the love, the caring, the joy of giving.

Continue to appreciate and bless the same person for as long as you wish. Or adopt a new mortal every week! Never reveal your identity. Then you can be assured that all the wonderful things you do for your adopted mortal are acts of pure unconditional love.

Suggested Reading

- *The Power of Unconditional Love: 21 Guidelines for Beginning, Improving, and Changing Your Most Meaningful Relationships,* by Ken Keyes Jr, presents a strategy for loving unconditionally. He suggests, "Unconditional love means learning to separate the person from the problem. Love the person; work with the problem."

- *Unconditional Love,* by John Powell, SJ, says, "Love is either conditional or unconditional. Either I attach conditions to my love for you or I do not. To the extent that I do attach such conditions, I do not really love you. I am only offering an exchange, not a gift. And true love is and must always be a free gift."

You Are!

We conclude this book the way we always ended the workshops we used to give together at the Findhorn Foundation, with the poem *You Are!* by William Arthur Ward, from the Unity publication, *You Are a Remarkable Person*. Do not be put off by the masculine pronouns (written long before the Age of Political Correctness); please allow yourself to resonate with the Spirit behind and beyond the words.

If God is... and He is!
If God is Love... and He is!
If you are made in His image... and you are!
Then you are Love.
You are a child of Love.
You are an expression of Love.
You are a channel of Love.
If God is... and He is!
If God is Truth... and He is!
If God lives in you... and He does!
Then you are Truth.
You are a child of Truth.
You are an expression of Truth.
You are a channel of Truth.
If God is... and He is!
If God is Wholeness... and He is!
If you are wholly of God... and you are!
Then you are Whole.
You are a child of Wholeness.
You are an expression of Wholeness.
You are a channel of Wholeness.

Once we experience for ourself the many benefits of bringing more *unconditional* love into our life and into the world, we celebrate the true freedom and joy of the Spirit.

Recommended Reading

Assagioli, MD, Roberto, *The Act of Will: A Guide to Self-Actualization and Self-Realization,* 1998, ISBN 0 9542915 0 6.

Augsburger, David, *Caring Enough to Confront,* 1979, ISBN 0 830702 56 3.

Caddy, Eileen, and Platts, PhD, David Earl, *Bringing More Love into Your Life: The Choice is Yours,* 1992, ISBN 0 905249 75 5.

Caddy, Eileen, and Platts, PhD, David Earl (ed.), *Opening Doors Within,* 2007, ISBN 978-1-94409-108-9.

Daily Word http://www.dailyword.com/

Ferrucci, Piero, *What We May Be: The Vision and Techniques of Psychosynthesis,* 1989, ISBN 1 852740 53 1.

Foundation for Inner Peace, *A Course in Miracles,* 1985 , ISBN 1 850630 16 X.

Gendlin, PhD, Eugene, *Focusing,* 1978, ISBN 0 896960 10 2.

Jampolsky, MD, Gerald, *Love is Letting Go of Fear,* 1979, ISBN 0 890872 46 5.

Jeffers, Susan, *Feel the Fear and Do It Anyway,* 1991, ISBN 0 099741008.

Keyes, Jr., Ken, *The Power of Unconditional Love: 21 Guidelines for Beginning, Improving and Changing Your Most Meaningful Relationships,* 1990, ISBN 0 915972 19 0.

Krystal, Phyllis, *Cutting the Ties That Bind,* 1993. ISBN pending.

Leonard, Jim, and Laut, Phil, *Vivation: The Science of Enjoying All Your Life,* 1990, ISBN 0 961013 24 9.

Ray, Sondra, *I Deserve Love: How Affirmations Can Guide You to Personal Fulfillment,* 1976, ISBN 0 890879 09 5.

Rowan, John. *Subpersonalities: The People Inside Us,* 1990, ISBN 0 415043 298.

Viscott, MD, David, *Risking,* 1977, ISBN 0 671626 90 6.

Wakefield, Dan, *The Story of Your Life: Writing a Spiritual Autobiography,* 1990, ISBN 0 807027 09 X.

About the Authors

EILEEN CADDY, MBE, (1917–2006) was a co-founder of the Findhorn Foundation with her husband Peter and colleague Dorothy Maclean. She is regarded by many as one of the most important mystics and spiritual teachers of the age and was awarded the MBE by the Queen in 2004, for 'services to spiritual inquiry'. Her books include *Opening Doors Within, God Spoke to Me, The Dawn of Change, Footprints on the Path, Waves of Spirit, The Spirit of Findhorn* and her acclaimed autobiography *Flight into Freedom and Beyond.*

Eileen believed strongly that the world needed unconditional love, and she had an inner prompting suggesting the greatest gift she could give people was to help them find their spiritual connection or God within themselves. So she dedicated her life to guiding people to explore deeply inside themselves by being quiet and listening quietly and expectantly until they came to experience their own divinity within.

DAVID EARL PLATTS, PhD, is an author, lecturer, and Psycho-synthesis trainer and counsellor who has been teaching and leading groups internationally for more than 35 years. In addition to the books and recordings he has done with Eileen Caddy, he has written *The Findhorn Book of Building Trust in Groups* and *Divinely Ordinary, Divinely Human: Celebrating the Life and Work of Eileen Caddy*. David also compiled and edited *Opening Doors Within*.

After careers in broadcasting and university work in the US, David travelled extensively in western Europe. He found his way to the Findhorn Foundation in Scotland where he lived and worked for eight years, and Findhorn slowly became his spiritual home.

He then moved to London to do a four-year professional counselling and therapy course at the Psychosynthesis and Education Trust where he learned methods for integrating the various parts of himself to provide a greater sense of wholeness—and for helping others to do the same.

Selected Titles by
Eileen Caddy

Opening Doors Within
God Spoke to Me
The Spirit of Findhorn
Flight into Freedom and Beyond
The Living Word
Footprints on the Path

Selected Titles on the
Findhorn Community

The Findhorn Garden Story by the Findhorn Community
Encounters with Nature Spirits by R. Ogilvie Crombie
Permaculture by Craig Gibsone & Jan Bang
Ecovillages around the World by Frederica Miller (ed.)

All available from www.findhornpress.com

The Findhorn Foundation is a dynamic experiment with a mission to transform human consciousness. Everyday life is guided by the inner voice of spirit, we work in co-creation with the intelligence of nature and take inspired action towards our vision of a better world.

We share our learning and way of life in experiential workshops, conferences and events.

For more information about this non-denominational experiential spiritual learning centre, ecovillage and community please visit our website.

www.findhorn.org

FINDHORN PRESS

Life-Changing Books

Learn more about us and our books at
www.findhornpress.com

For information on the Findhorn Foundation:
www.findhorn.org